# THOMAS CLARKSON

NEGRO ENLANC

THOMAS CLARKSON

H. ANELAY.

J. JOHNSTON.

# THOMAS CLARKSON:

## A Monograph.

BEING

## A CONTRIBUTION TOWARDS THE HISTORY OF THE ABOLITION OF THE SLAVE-TRADE AND SLAVERY.

BY

## JAMES ELMES,

AUTHOR OF "A HISTORICAL, SCIENTIFIC, AND COMMERCIAL SURVEY OF THE PORT
OF LONDON;" "TREATISE ON ECCLESIASTICAL AND CIVIL DILAPIDATIONS;"
"HORÆ VACIVÆ;" "SIR CHRISTOPHER WREN AND HIS TIMES;"
ETC., ETC., ETC.

---

"One, who in Freedom's noble cause,
Has brav'd th' oppressor's ire,
And pleaded truth's and virtue's laws
With zeal that could not tire."
BERNARD BARTON, *on a Portrait of Clarkson.*

---

## LONDON:

BLACKADER AND CO., 13, PATERNOSTER ROW.
1854.

Reprinted by Mnemosyne Publishing Co., Inc. Miami, Florida

LONDON:
PRINTED BY WALTON AND MITCHELL
WARDOUR ST., OXFORD ST.

**First Mnemosyne reprinting 1969**

**Reprinted from a copy in the
Fisk University Library Negro Collection.**

Copyright © 1969    Mnemosyne Publishing Co., Inc.    Miami, Florida

Library of Congress Catalog Card Number:
76-89414

Printed in the United States of America

TO

# THE RIGHT HON. ASHLEY COOPER,

## Earl of Shaftesbury, Baron Ashley,

ETC., ETC., ETC.

---

My Lord,—

EXAMPLES set by persons in high places, are productive of good or evil, in proportion to the good or evil qualities displayed by the exemplars ; because example is a strong motive power upon the actions of men, and necessarily leads to imitation.

The author of "The Book of Wisdom," written in the name of the royal sage of Judah, says, "When virtue is present, men take example thereat ; and if it go away, yet they desire it ; it is always crowned and triumpheth, and winneth the battle and the undefiled reward."*

---

* Ch. iv., ver. 2.

That example in high places produces imitation in those of lower degree, either in age, station or intellect, who again find imitators down to the lowest and most servile of our race, is shewn in every page of history, from the obsequious courtiers of Roman vice and tyranny, who stiffened their necks, and wryed their heads, in base imitation of the torquillated Caligula, the present god of their obscene idolatry, to the beauties of England, who ruffed and yoked themselves to the chin, because their royal mistress, Elizabeth, had not a spotless neck; and, to descend to more recent times, when the handsome youth of England betowelled their throats up to the ears, and rose their coat-collars to the crown of their heads, because their rising sun, the handsome Prince of Wales, had not a neck like the Apollo of the Belvedere. To gain favour in those days, a man must have aped the style and manners of the Jockey Club; or, as an anonymous satirist of that day said,

" I will caress some noblemen of note,
And imitate his language and his coat."*

* *The Man of Taste*, a Satire.

Examples, like seed, producing good or evil fruit, are to be found abundantly in sacred history. There we find how the people were made righteous or infamous by the example of their princes. "Jeroboam, the son of Nebat, who made Israel to sin," is a perpetual running commentary upon the maxim, "*Iter per præcepta longum est, breve et efficax per exempla.*"*

But there are many shining examples on the higher and the brighter side, which led the people to virtue, wisdom, happiness and honour. "The idea and the *exemplar* in the world was first in GOD," says our thoughtful historian of the world;† and those who have approached the nearest to that unapproachable eminence, have been at once the happiest followers and the greatest leaders.

By following such precepts, and by setting such examples, did the illustrious triumvirate of philanthropists, whose acts shed honour on their country, produce such a distinguished legion of willing colleagues, and cohorts of active allies.

---

* Sen. *Ep.* † Sir Walter Raleigh.

Thus did Granville Sharp, the grandson of an exemplary prelate, lead his brother jurists to proclaim through " silvered-tongued Murray,"* the golden dictate, that "a slave coming into Great Britain, becomes *ipso facto* FREE." This sentiment or judgment was pronounced in the name of the whole bench; and declares, in so many words, that by the laws of GOD, and of our realm, slavery breaks its bonds on touching British soil.

Thus also did Thomas Clarkson, a gentleman by birth, and a divine by ordination, produce laudable imitation, and lead his colleagues of the Society of Friends to support his righteous cause, to give freedom to their own slaves, and to recommend their example to be followed by the whole of their brotherhood, till, in the year 1787, there was not a slave in the possession of an acknowledged Quaker.†

---

* Earl of Mansfield, Chief Justice of England.

† See the examples followed and set by David and John Barclay, grandsons of Robert Barclay of Urie, the distinguished author of the "Apology for the true Christian Divinity, as the same is preached and held forth, by the people in scorn

And thus, again, did William Wilberforce,
also a gentleman by birth, a man of wealth by
honourable patrimony, a man of fashion by education and association, a Christian by conviction,
the father and preceptor of distinguished sons,
put vice and folly to the blush, taught the great
to set better examples to the less, prevailed on
the Government to issue the celebrated Royal
Proclamation against vice and immorality, and
founded the Society for the Reformation of Manners for carrying its measures into effect; and,
if the expression be not profane, brought religion into fashion.  He published his *Practical
Christianity* amidst political turmoil, parliamentary labours and London life.  Its effect upon
the higher classes was prodigious, and it spread
among the people a beneficial influence.

---

called Quakers," who, after speaking against slavery in the
society to which Mr. Clarkson belonged, and after the beginning
of his public labours, had property demised to them in Jamaica,
upon which were two and thirty slaves. Convinced of the crime
of holding fellow men in bondage, they emancipated them all,
and sent an agent to Jamaica in 1795 for that purpose; provided
situations for the adults, trades for the youths, and school-
learning for those of younger age.

Before this man of peace, Pitt vailed his commanding brow and lofty head, and Tierney shrunk
in silence, when he, the only man in the House
of Commons who dared to mention it, announced
his intention of bringing before the House their
barbarous desecration of the Sabbath, by fighting
a duel in the hour of divine worship.

Burke, the impassioned orator, the eloquent
rhetorician, the enlightened statesman, the
leader of a ten years' suit against an eastern
oppressor, having prepared a bill for the regula-
tion of the slave-trade, despairing of carrying
its abolition; " declared that, when he found
Mr. Wilberforce had seriously undertaken the
work, and that his motion was for the abolition,
which he approved much more than his own,
burnt his papers, and made an offering of them
in honour of his nobler proposition; much in
the same manner as we read, that the curious
books were offered up and burnt at the approach
of the Gospel."*    Such were among the results
of good exemplars.

---

* Woodfall's Reports, April 19th, 1792.

The good example set to the world, in Dr. Woodward's *History of the Society for the Reformation of Manners, in the year* 1692, had an acknowledged effect upon the reviver of the Society in 1787, as did Robert Nelson's *Address to Persons of Quality*, in Queen Anne's reign, on the *Practical Christianity*, in that of George III. Such are a few of the many beneficial effects of good example.

I trust your Lordship will pardon the length of my unsubmitted dedication, which I have done solely on public grounds ; for as a reader of English history, and acknowledging that although political freedom is a great blessing, personal freedom is a greater, I am reminded that we owe that great national palladium, the Habeas Corpus Act, to an Earl of Shaftesbury ; that to another of the same distinguished title literature is indebted, among other moral and philosophical works, for the *Characteristics of Men, Manners, Opinions and Times*, and for *The Moralists*, which Bishop Hurd pronounces to be one of the most finished productions, on the Platonic model, in the English language. Here are examples worthy of imitation; nor has your Lordship failed, either as a representative of the people in the Commons' House of Parliament, as a peer of the realm in the Upper House, and, as an untiring philanthropist in the world, from setting a great example to the British people.

With these feelings of respect and honour,

I have the honour to be,

Your Lordship's very obedient Servant,

JAMES ELMES.

*London, January 1st, 1854.*

# PREFACE.

THIS memoir is not a biography of Mr. Clarkson. The performance of that duty belongs more properly to a relative or to a personal friend of that wise, zealous and untiring advocate of the rights and privileges of mankind. It is, however, intended to be a sketch of that portion of his long and patriotic life, which he religiously devoted to the extrication of his country from the taint of that accursed thing, which reduced the mighty commonwealth of Rome to a tyrannic empire, and that great but vicious empire to the dominion of bigoted and superstitious despots over a nation of slaves. Tyranny and slavery are reciprocal terms, nay, perhaps synonymous; for tyrants are slaves to their passions, and to their wretched favourites; and their miserable subjects are slaves to them all. From Julius the Dictator to Augustus the Emperor, was a great decline in the political and personal liberty of the Romans; but what a fall from Augustus to Tiberius, and even from that dissimulating hypocrite to the madman Nero, and downwards in the road to destruction, through the insanities of Caligula, and Domitian, and Caracalla, and Commodus and Heliogabalus, apes of cruelty and monsters of depravity. These emperors were slave-owners. May not the horrifying cruelties of the slave-dealers and slave-owners of the last century, and of the present day,— Englishmen, who have purged themselves from the guilt; Americans, north and south, of whom there are hopes; Spaniards and Portuguese and Cubans, steeped to the lips in barbarity.

Let the admirers of the self-called "model Republic," turn to the records of that state whence they borrowed their "Cincinnati" and their "Capitol." There they will find the great republican General, the treacherous subverter of the liberties of his country, when writing upon the sacred word "Libertas," tells the admiring world the following truism, "*Omnes homines naturâ libertati studere, et odisse conditionem servitorum;"* and yet this republican leader was at once a slave-owner, a slave-dealer, and a slave-maker. His wives were his slaves, his children were his property; he was absolute master of all within his walls, and would have been master of the world, had not Brutus slain him at the base of Pompey's statue. Nay, his favourite concubine, the mother of that very Brutus, bore the appropriate name of Servitia. Slaves served him in his gilded halls; slaves ministered to all his wants and desires; slaves wove his textile robes; slaves chased the fibulæ of his buskins, and the laurel wreath that concealed his baldness; slaves moulded and carved his statues and his busts; his servile senate were slaves; slaves served him in his legions, and were slaughtered by millions in his murderous wars; ten thousand slaves fought as gladiators in the bloody arena, for the amusement of the millions of slaves who lived indolently and ingloriously under his rule; and a greater slave than all offered him the imperial diadem. But a stern

---

* J. Cæsar, *Comm.*, lib. iii.

eye surveyed him from without, and the eye of conscience glared fearfully upon him from within.

Mr. Fox cannot be accused of an overweening love for the insanity of arbitrary power, nor of hatred to republican institutions, and let these transatlantic Republicans attend to his words: "Where could be found," asks this eloquent enemy of slavery, *negro* slavery, "finer sentiments of liberty than in Demosthenes and Cicero? Where bolder assertions of the rights of mankind than in Tacitus and Thucydides? But, alas! these were the holders of slaves."* So, alas! are the orators and statesmen, the historians and soldiers, the philosophers and, shame to the name, some of the divines, of the great transatlantic Republic! Attend again; but, in reading, *dele* "Great Britain," and insert "America:" "The trade is defensible on no other principle than that of a highwayman. Great Britain cannot keep it upon those terms. Mere gain is not a motive for a great country

---

* Mr. Fox's speech in the House of Commons, against slavery and slave trading, April 18th, 1791.

to rest on, as a justification of any measure. Honour is its superior; and justice is superior to honour."

Slaves swarmed in every Grecian state, as in more modern states, which cry aloud for freedom. Attica has been computed to have numbered nearly half a million of slaves; in the single island of Ægina were four hundred and seventy thousand of these wretched beings; and the civilized city of Corinth had nearly as many.

In Rome the slaves were numbered by legions, by armies, by cohorts. The noblest of the Roman knights, senators and orators, brawlers for freedom, kept slaves to traffic in their offspring, like a Southdown sheep-breeder. Let Horace tell how safely these magnates lived amidst those armies of unwilled men; read what he says to Mæcenas:

" An vigilare metu exanimen, noclésque diésque
  Formidare malos fures, incendia, servos,
  Ne te compilent fugientes : hoc juvat ?"*

He asks his patrician friend if he knows the *real* value of wealth. Is it, he asks, to watch, half-

---

* Lib. i., sat. i., 76.

dead with fear, by night and by day, in dread of profligate thieves, fire, and *your slaves*, lest they should run away and plunder you; is not this, he asks, delightful? What say you, men of Carolina and New Orleans, or the brother-lovers of Philadelphia? Four hundred slaves, belonging to Pedanius Secundus, were put to death, in order to get rid of them, on suspicion of being concerned in the assassination of their master! Pollio, a friend of Augustus, fed the carp and other favourite fish of the Roman epicures with the flesh of slaves, whom he had butchered for the purpose, with as little remorse as the ducal Lord of Arundel, a quarter of a century ago, fed his horned owls with the flesh of the young King Charles's spaniels, rather than increase the rare breed by giving them to his friends. In like manner did a planter,* who had succeeded in recovering a runaway slave, command his surgeon to amputate the man's leg, to prevent a recurrence of the offence; and when the humane man refused, the master smashed his

---

* Related, among other atrocities, by Mr. Fox in his before-quoted speech.

slave's leg, fractured the bones, and said, "Now, sir, do your duty; amputate the leg, and save the nigger's life."

Cato declared, that their slaves were their enemies; and a common Roman proverb said, "So many slaves, so many enemies." Seneca* warns his countrymen, "to recall the examples of those masters who have perished in domestic snares, either by treachery or force; and you will learn that *the vengeance of slaves numbers not fewer victims than that of tyrants.*" Look at the infuriated successors of these slaves, when they ravaged, sacked, and pillaged imperial Rome, glutting their savage vengeance; and, in our times, when the white slaves of France burst their bonds, and filled Europe with a flame, not yet extinguished.

Horace, again,† compares his ease of mind, arising from the few cares of his frugal estate, with the terrors of the rich; he laughs at losses, *flights of slaves*, and fires:

"Detrimenta, *fugas servorum*, incendia redet."

---

* Ep. iv., 6.　　　† Lib. ii., Ep. i., 121.

And in the before-quoted Ode, he says he should always wish to be very poor in possessions held upon such terms:

"Horum
Semper ego optâtim pauperimus esse bonorum."

### With like feeling our Cowper sung:

"I would not have a slave to till my ground,
To carry me, to fan me while I sleep,
And tremble when I wake, for all the wealth
That sinews bought and sold have ever earned."

Martial* records, with fear, the number of the slaves in Rome; and Juvenal† complains, with Horace, of the cares of the rich and the fears of the wealthy, as to this artificial, heartless commodity of slaves:

"Tantis parta malis, cura majore metuque
Servantur, Misera est magni custodia census,
Dispositis prædives hamis vigilare cohortem
Servorum noctu Licinus jubet, attonitus pro
Electro, signisque suis," etc.

In enumerating the slave population of Rome, emphatically enslaved and enslaving Rome—

---

* Sat. i., iii., 11.          † Sat., xiv., 303.

which amounted to nearly half its population—
from the day when Cæsar, Pompey, and Crassus
divided the mighty commonwealth, the Roman
world, among them, down to the hour when
republican France, under her thrice-perjured
dictator; imperial Austria, under her slavish
government; and Pius IX., invested and divested
of a slave's livery, divided or rather supported
the mongrel capital of paganized Christendom,
till the day of division shall arrive, the genus
and species of the races deserve consideration.

First were the senators and knights, and
their senatorial slaves; medicoes, painters, wits,
buffoons, dressers, musicians, parasites, poets,
dramatists, mimics, and such like appendages to
the luxuries of the great; to say nothing of the
more infamous contributors to their enjoyments,
which the historians, orators, and satirists de-
scribe with fearful veracity. Then were the
foreigners and their slaves, of which more com-
plaints are made than against the home-bred
slaves of Rome. We can manage our own
breed, say they, but have no control over the
vices and the crimes of the imported stock.

Next were the soldiers, and, if in the depth a deeper hell be found, their slaves. Slaves to slaves! Then we find the plebeians, and—their slaves; and, above or below all, the public or state slaves, amounting, according to the German historian Höck,* to 940,000 slaves, out of a population of 2,265,000 of nominally freemen.

Slavery in Rome and slavery in America, are of equal infamy and equal terror, not only to the families which own them, but to the state. Vettius, a Roman knight, brought into danger by his voluptuous indulgences and criminal extravagance, and deeply in debt, descended from his equestrian rank to that of a demagogue, and armed out of his own household four hundred slaves, and raised a revolt. The higher order of slaves suppressed the insurrection, and the would-be hero was punished as a traitor. Conspiracies and plots among the slaves, to murder their masters, fire the capitol, destruction by false accusation, poison and the dagger, sully the Roman history from five centuries be-

---

* In his *Römische Geschicte*, vol. i., part ii., p. 400.

fore the Christian era, through the servile wars,
down to the terrible retribution by the Goths
and Vandals, the descendants of the slaves who
fought as gladiators for the amusement of Roman dames and senators.  Every Roman mansion and villa had a prison for rebellious and
erring slaves; and in so little estimation was
human life held by these polished barbarians,
that Q. Flaminius, a Roman senator, slew one of
his slaves to gratify a guest who had never seen
a man put to death.  The law of property in the
slave, as far as concerned the owner, was as correctly defined among the ancient Romans as
among the modern Americans; and restitution
was made for injury or death, not to the sufferer
or his family, but to his owner.  Translate a
speech from a comedy of Plautus* into English,
and it will read like one of Uncle Tom's.
"Blows are continually falling on my shoulders;
the whip is always at work; I am sent into the
country to slave for the family there; when my
master sups abroad, I have to carry a torch be-

---

* Captiv. ii., i. 133.

fore him; by my labours I have earned a right
to freedom, and I am growing grey in slavery."

Seneca relates that, on one occasion, it was
proposed in the Roman senate to give a distinctive dress to the slaves, that they might be
known; but it was rejected on the ground that
it would be dangerous to give them the means
of counting their masters. The American
senate have no need to propose or repudiate
such a proposition; for nature has given the
distinctive mark, and the dark and swarthy can
count the white and yellow.

Men of America! a civil war raised you to
liberty; beware, lest a servile war does not re-
store a race to liberty, from a more galling
despotism than your forefathers ever dreamed
of. You were tyrannized over as colonists, by
your mother country; but you were never considered as saleable goods and chattels, and as
men without human existence. Beware, lest
some bold Spartacus, from among your hated
and feared "vagabonds,"* mount your capitol,

---

* Spartacum vagantem, *Hor.*, lib. iii., carm. xiv. 19.

and call upon his race to avenge their wrongs, in words of electric fire.

"Arise, ye slaves, and glut your vengeful ire!"

I am not alone in fearing that nothing but such a servile outbreak will cause slavery to be abolished in America. Remember the servile war in Rome, and fear with Horace lest the victorious barbarians trample upon the ashes of your cities, and insultingly disperse the bones of your Romulus. Remember the maroons in Jamaica, and the black Spartacus of Hayti.

Before the blow be struck, imagine some milder spirit addressing you behind that coloured skin, which you despise and spurn:

> "Is there, as you sometimes tell us,
>    Is there One who rules on high;
> Has He bid you buy and sell us,
>    Speaking from His throne, the sky?
> Ask Him if your knotted scourges,
>    Fetters, blood-extorting screws,
> Are the means which duty urges
>    Agents of His will to use?
>         *    *    *    *
> Slaves of gold! whose sordid dealings
>    Tarnish all your boasted powers,

> Prove that you have human feelings
> Ere you proudly question ours."*

Thinking men of America, you of " the upper ten thousand," wise spirits of the new world, the salt that is to savour your future institutions, look at the two pictures which the land of your forefathers, the land whence you derived your origin, your language, your institutes of law and religion, and make your selection. Freedom or slavery? A state cannot be free, where a fearful portion of its population is held in bondage by the alarmed and affrighted other part, who for a time bear a timid sway.

> " But change their servile hate, to legal fear,
> And filial love."

Attend, ye professors of freedom, to the malediction of one† of the greatest lovers of freedom that ever wrote in the freeman's native tongue :

> " O execrable son! so to aspire
> Above his brethren; to himself assuming
> Authority usurpt from God not giv'n ;

---

* Cowper.                † Milton.

He gave us only, over beast, fish, fowl,
Dominion absolute; that right we hold
By His donation: but man over men
He made not lord; such title to Himself
Reserving, human left from human free."

Pursuant to this divine command—for the bard of paradise drew his inspiration from the word of God—it is our pride and boast:

" Slaves cannot breathe in England; if their lungs
Receive our air, that moment they are free;*
They touch our country, and their shackles fall.
That's noble and bespeaks a nation proud
And jealous of the blessing. Spread it then,
And let it circulate through every vein
Of all your country.†

Anthony Benezet, a distinguished philanthropist of America, in the year 1767, sent across the broad Atlantic a friendly caution to Great Britain and her colonies, on the calamitous state of the enslaved negroes in her dominions; which produced a beneficial effect in this country, as demonstrated in the following pages.‡ Let

---

* See the trial of Somerset *v.* Stewart, pp. 27, 33, 37, and 41, of this work.

† Cowper.      ‡ See page 67.

therefore an English lover of humanity, in grateful return, offer an equally sincere caution to his friends on the western side of the Atlantic ocean.

Another intention of this work is to serve as an introduction to a general history of the rise, progress and abolition of the slave-trade and slavery by the British people, as an example worthy of all imitation, by similar offenders against the laws of GOD, and of humanity. This fact, although so recent, seems almost forgotten by the generation who witnessed it, and unknown to the young and rising of our race; and this sketch of its destruction may excite a desire to know more of a traffic which it was the infamy of one English government to create and legalize, and the glory of the united British people, in our age, to destroy.

The materials for this history were collected, partly arranged, and the work begun. But as it must occupy much time to complete it, it was laid aside, and the following cantlet, from the stock of collected facts, produced as a contribution, after the manner of the French *Memoires pour servir a l'Histoire*, etc., towards that history. But it is more particularly intended as an honest chronicle of the zealous, indefatigable and persevering labours, faithful to the end, of that distinguished triumvirate of friends, Sharp, Clarkson and Wilberforce, to whose meritorious exertions the universal world is indebted for this great tribute to religion and humanity. Clarkson, alone of the three, lived to see the end of the work; and his last public act, was to present himself at the bar of the Upper House, to present a petition to the legislature in favour of an extension of the great object of his life, to countries who still close their eyes to its justice and its blessings.

Clarkson has been charged by contemporary reviewers and others, with vanity, egotism, and self-exaltation.* In reading his account of the transaction, nothing can be more fair and liberal towards all his colleagues and helpmates; and his affectionate and grateful feelings towards

---

* See the Rev. Ch. Ign. Latrobe's letter to his daughter, in *The Life of William Wilberforce*, by his Sons, p. 77.

those eminent men, Messrs. Granville Sharp and Wilberforce, is strongly illustrated in his conversation with Haydon, whilst sitting for his portrait, quoted towards the end of this work.

Precedent will not make vice, virtue; but it is yet to be proved that this strong sense of their own sufficiency, common to all men of genius, be a vice. In favour of this strong sense of self-sufficency, there are many and mighty precedents. Does not Horace promise to himself an immortality of fame from his poetry, which he calls a monument more lasting than bronze, more sublime than the lofty regal pyramids, which neither the wasting rain, the impotent north wind, nor innumerable ages, shall be able to demolish?*   And does not Ovid similarly boast that even the wrath of Jove himself shall not destroy his works? Does not Milton boast,

" Myself I thought born to promote all Truth,
  All righteous things."†

---

* Lib. iii., Od. 30.
† In his verses on his school-life.

Hogarth boasted to Reynolds, that when his *Marriage a-la-Mode* came out he should gratify the world with a sight they had never seen equalled; Buffon, says Mr. D'Israeli,* wrote his own panegyric, beneath his statue in the library of the *Jardin des Plantes*, and asserted of the great geniuses of modern ages, "there are but five, Bacon, Newton, Liebnitz, Montesquieu, and MYSELF." Our Bishop Watson felt such a strong consciousness of his powers, and that whatever he did he did in his best manner, as a master in his art; and whatever he wrote he declared was the best work on the subject. "When I am dead," said our first and greatest professor of anatomy in the Royal Academy, "you will not soon meet with another John Hunter." Kepler, the planetary legislator, was no self-abaser, but boldly proclaims, "I dare insult mankind by confessing that I am he who has turned science to advantage. If I am pardoned I shall rejoice; if blamed, I shall endure it. The die is cast, I have written this book; and whether it be read by posterity, or by my

---

* Well versified in his *Curiosities of Literature.*

contemporaries, is of no consequence. It may well wait for a reader during one century, when GOD Himself, during six thousand years, has not sent an observer like myself." His discoveries have been verified, and he stands aloft in the midst of the brightest geniuses of his times. " EGO, *et rex meus*," said Wolsey; and who doubts the pre-eminence, be it for good or evil? But why multiply instances, when the half of those which now crowd upon my memory would fill a book? Shakspeare says,

> " Self-love is not so vile a sin
> As self-neglecting."*

Milton defends what he practised, and affirms that,

> " Nothing profits more
> Than self-esteem, grounded on just and right,
> Well manag'd."†

But a greater authority than these proclaims self-love to be the greatest and the strongest of human affections; and commands, " Thou shalt love thy neighbour as THYSELF."‡

---

* *Henry the Fifth.*      † *Paradise Lost.*      ‡ Matt. xxii. 39.

# THOMAS CLARKSON.

# THOMAS CLARKSON,
## A MONOGRAPH.

### CHAPTER I.

"To deal and traffic in human flesh and blood, not in the labour of men, is to devour the root instead of enjoying the fruit of human diligence."—BURKE.

INTRODUCTION—FIRST RISE OF THE SUBJECT OF THE SLAVE TRADE AND SLAVERY IN MR. CLARKSON'S MIND—A BRIEF SKETCH OF THE LITERARY AND LEGAL STATE OF THE CASE PREVIOUSLY THERETO—MR. CLARKSON OBTAINS THE FIRST PRIZE FROM THE VICE-CHANCELLOR AT CAMBRIDGE—HIS FEELINGS ON THE SUBJECT DURING HIS STUDIES AND ON HIS JOURNEY FROM THE UNIVERSITY HOMEWARDS—PUBLISHES HIS PRIZE ESSAY—IS INTRODUCED TO SOME FRIENDS OF THE ABOLITION OF THE SLAVE TRADE—MAKES A PLEDGE TO DEDICATE HIMSELF EXCLUSIVELY TO ITS ABOLITION—RETURNS TO LONDON—BEGINS THE PURSUIT OF ABOLITION AS THE BUSINESS OF HIS LIFE.

THERE is not a more delightful and heart-cheering pursuit, than that of following the track of a good man engaged in the cause of humanity; and of witnessing indefatigable perseverance in benevolence, against legions of opponents, to which inferior minds would have succumbed. No man ever engaged in a more righteous cause than did young THOMAS CLARKSON, when he devoted all the energies of his vigorous and robust body, to the exclusion of almost every other consideration, to wage war against the traffickers in the flesh and blood of human beings : nor did any one who joined him in his heaven-directed mission, put forth more fervent zeal, fearless courage and untiring perseverance, in combatting the swarthy demons of the African slave-trade, than did the youthful leader of this philanthropic band of Christian brothers.

Great effects have often sprung from little causes; a fish-bone caused the death of Tarquinius Priscus, a fly that of Adrian IV., and a hair in a drink of milk terminated the earthly career of Fabius Pictor; so did a College Essay by an Undergraduate of Cambridge, lead to the glorious abolition of the African slave-trade by the whole Christian world, and the extinction of slavery throughout the entire British Empire. Worthily did our great modern poet, Wordsworth, apostrophize this indomitable man, when he exclaimed,

> " True yoke-fellow of Time,
> With unabated effort, see, the palm
> Is won, and by all nations shall be worn."*

That which Burke feared to attempt, and even abandoned, after drawing out a code of regulations for the immediate mitigation and subsequent abolition of slavery, from the conviction that the strength of the West India body would defeat the utmost efforts of his powerful party, and cover them with ruinous unpopularity, Clarkson and his holy brotherhood accomplished. The simple circumstance of a University annual prize dissertation, to which the Vice-Chancellor's attention had been attracted by circumstances hereinafter mentioned, led the way, under GOD, to the abolition of the horrid

---

* Sonnet to Thomas Clarkson.

traffic in human flesh and blood, by the British Parliament.

Mr. Clarkson has given, in his *History of the Abolition of the Slave Trade*, an interesting piece of autobiography, to which he was in a manner forced by the entreaty of friends, after having declined the task of historiographer of the abolition, on the ground that he could not undertake it without making himself too prominent in the scenes or omitting much of the truth, and thus render himself obnoxious to the charge of self-glorying and vanity, of sounding his own praise. Cæsar was unwilling to write his own Commentaries; but Clarkson yielded, and produced a series of historical documents of this great national event, the truth of which none have doubted, although his fears were justified by the attacks of envious contemporaries.

To these objections his friends replied that he might treat the proposed history as a sort of biographical memoir towards a general account of the great work, or as a sketch of his labours in the righteous cause; hinting that many persons who had less weighty matters to communicate had written their own memoirs, yet no one had charged them with vanity or egotism for so doing. Cæsar magnifies himself for the murder of millions; Clarkson glories in contributing to the restoration of millions of degraded slaves to their birthright as men and brethren.

This reasoning moved him, and he determined, in compliance with their wishes, to examine his objections carefully. Having performed his promise, and given satisfactory reasons for his compliance, he undertook the task of being the honest chronicler of the important transactions in which he took such a distinguished part. He was desirous, above all, to attribute his exertions to the uncontrollable influence of a Superior Power moving within him. "The power of Him," he says, "who gave me a heart to feel, who gave me courage to begin, and perseverance to proceed. I am thankful to Him, with the greatest feeling of humility, for having permitted me to become useful in any degree to my fellow-creatures."

With this modest—this truly Christian feeling of universal benevolence, did Clarkson begin his valuable memoir. From the scattered heaps of facts dispersed in his authentic pages is collected the following connected narrative of his personal labours and unceasing exertions, in evil report and good report, fearless of that "ruinous unpopularity" which scared Burke from his good intentions, in fatigues and dangers of body, perturbations of mind, malicious insinuations and pointed scorn, till the battle was won and the victory proclaimed. The end of this contribution towards the history of the abolition of the slave trade and slavery, is to show in a condensed form, the indefatigable and almost unexampled exertions which Mr. Clarkson used for so many years to remove this stigma from our nation.

In the year 1785, when Mr. Clarkson was in the

class of senior wrangler in the University of Cambridge, the Vice-Chancellor gave out two subjects for the Latin dissertations; one to the Middle Bachelors, and the other to the Senior Bachelors of Arts. To the latter he propounded the following subject,—which, from the important results that flowed from it, ought, together with the name of the reverend author, to be inscribed in letters of gold.

"ANNE LICEAT INVITOS IN SERVITUTEM DARE?" Is it lawful to make slaves of others against their will? The proposition of this important inquiry was made, as before mentioned, by the Vice-Chancellor of the University of Cambridge—the honoured and valued Rev. J. Peckard, D.D., who had distinguished himself in the earlier part of his life, by some publications on the intermediate state of the soul between the death of the body and its resurrection, and some others in favour of civil and religious liberty. During the time that he was Master of Magdalen College, it devolved upon him in 1784 to preach a sermon before the University. In this discourse he spoke of the slave trade in the following appropriate terms.

"Now, whether we consider the crime with respect to the individuals concerned in this most barbarous and cruel traffic, or whether we consider it as patronized and encouraged by the laws of the land, it presents to our view an equal degree of enormity. A crime, founded on a dreadful preeminence in wickedness ; a crime, which being both of individuals and of the nation, must some time draw down upon us the heaviest judgment of Almighty GOD, who made of one blood all the sons of men, and who gave to all equally a natural right to liberty, and who, ruling all the kingdoms of the earth with equal providential justice, cannot suffer such deliberate, such monstrous iniquity to pass long unpunished."

When this benevolent and patriotic divine was raised to the Vice-Chancellorship of his University, he took the first opportunity that presented itself of exciting the attention of the public to the crimes which he had denounced from the pulpit, by the instrumentality of a University Prize, addressed to the young and ardent minds of the under-graduates.

The attention of the Vice-Chancellor had doubtlessly been called to this great national crime, by a kindred spirit, Granville Sharp, who in 1769 had published *A representation of the Injustice and Dangerous Tendency of tolerating Slavery, or of admitting the least Claim of Private Property in the Persons of Men in England*. This work, by a sound constitutional lawyer, was in answer to an opinion given in 1729 by the (then) Attorney-General, Sir Philip Yorke,* and Solicitor-General, the Hon. Charles Talbot,† concerning the case of slaves in Great Britain. This eminent philanthropist also published in 1776 a little work from which the Vice-Chancellor, judging from internal evidence,

---

* Afterwards Lord Chancellor and first Earl of Hardwicke.

† Afterwards Lord Chancellor Talbot; honoured after his death by the dedication of the first stanza of Thompson's Poem of *Liberty*, to his memory.

must have gained some legal information. It is called* *The Law of Liberty*, or as it is called in Scripture by way of eminence† νομον βασιλικον— *The Royal Law*, by which all mankind will certainly be judged. This tract was specially addressed to the serious consideration of all slave holders and slave dealers. Another of this gentleman's publications appears to have guided a portion of Dr. Peckard's arguments. This was also published in 1776, and is entitled, *The Law of Retribution; or, a serious Warning to Great Britain and her Colonies; founded on unquestionable Examples of God's temporal Vengeance against Tyrants, Slave-holders and Oppressors.* He also published and distributed largely several other tracts against this enormous crime, before the Vice-Chancellor called the attention of the university and the country to its serious consideration.

The examples cited in the last-mentioned of these pamphlets, are selected from predictions in the Old

---

* James ii. 12.     † James ii. 8.

Testament, of national judgments which, being compared with the actual accomplishment, demonstrate
" the sure word of prophecy," as well as the immediate interposition of divine Providence to recompense
impenitent nations, by retribution, according to their
works. A singular parallelism between those distinguished expositors of " The Royal Law" occurs,
wherein the Rev. Vice-Chancellor from the University pulpit, in 1781, calls the slave trade " a crime
founded on a dreadful pre-eminence in wickedness :
a crime, which being both of individuals and of the
nation, must, some time, draw down upon us the
heaviest judgment of Almighty GOD, who made of
one blood all the sons of men, and who gave to all
equally a natural right to liberty:"—and the missive
on the Royal Law of Liberty, from the learned Jurist
to the slave-holders and slave-dealers of Great Britain and its colonies, wherein he writes from the Old
Jewry in 1776 : " The African slave trade, which
includes the most contemptuous violation of *brotherly
love* and *charity* that men can be guilty of, *is openly*

*encouraged and promoted by the* BRITISH PARLIA-
MENT ! and the most detestable and oppressive slavery
that ever disgraced even the unenlightened heathens,
is notoriously tolerated in the British Colonies, by
the public Acts of their respective assemblies ; by
Acts that have been *ratified by the assent and concurrence of* BRITISH KINGS !"*

But Granville Sharp was born an advocate of the
Royal Law of Liberty, and of the abolition of the
" accursed thing"—*Slavery.* It ran in his blood ;
his grandfather, John Sharp, Archbishop of York,
who suffered persecution for conscience, from James
II., received the archiepiscopal *pallium* from William
III., and preached the coronation sermon for Queen

---

* By an Act of Virginia, which received the royal assent in
the 4th of Anne, ch. xlix., sec. 37, it is enacted, " that after
proclamation is issued against slaves that run away and lie out,
*it is lawful for any person whatsoever to kill and destroy such
slaves, by such means as he, she, or they shall think fit ; without accusation or impeachment of any crime for the same ;*
and much more of the same diabolical tendency ; and other
similar Acts, with *royal assent,* in our other colonies.

Anne, who appointed him her grand almoner. This learned and eloquent prelate, in a Sermon* preached before the House of Commons, April 11, 1769, warned our great national council of GOD's vengeance against such atrocious crimes ; and told them boldly and emphatically, "That Africa which is not now more fruitful of monsters than it was once of excellently wise and learned men ; that Africa, which formerly afforded us our *Clemens,* our *Origen,* our *Tertullian,* our *Cyprian,* our *Augustine,* and many other extraordinary lights in the church of God ; that *famous Africa, in whose soil Christianity did thrive prodigiously, and could boast of so many flourishing churches, alas ! is now a wilderness.* 'The wild boars have broken into the vineyard and eaten it up, and it brings forth nothing but briars and thorns,' to use the words of the prophet ; and who knows but GOD may suddenly make this *church and nation, this our England,* which, Jeshurun-like, is waxed

---

* See Archbishop Sharp's *Sermons.* 7 vols. 8vo. London. 1715. Vol. II., p. 22.

fat and grown proud, and has kicked against GOD, *such another example of the vengeance of this kind ?"*

The despised, enslaved, branded, pillaged Africans, Ethiopians or negroes, received and embraced Christianity much earlier than the Europeans. Among the earliest Gentile converts to Christianity in the apostolic age is the African Prince,* treasurer to Candace, Queen of the Ethiopians, who was baptized by Philip the Apostle, and received the Holy Ghost. Ancient traditions relate that this illustrious convert preached the Gospel in his own country, and baptized his royal mistress, who was the first fruit of his mission. It is also recorded that he proceeded to preach the glad tidings in the neighbouring country of Abyssinia, in Arabia Felix and

---

* The passage, ἀνὴ Αἰθίοψ, εὐνοῦχος δυνάστης Κανδάκης τῆς Βασιλίσσης Αἰθιόπων, " a man of Ethiopia, an eunuch of great authority under Candace, Queen of the Ethiopians," should be rather *a chamberlain*, being derived from εὐνὴ *cubile,* and ἐχω *servo,* and not necessarily a *castrato.* Δυναστης also, is a Lord or Prince.

in Ceylon. Job Ludolf or Lutholf, a learned oriental scholar of Erfurt in the seventeenth century, in his *Historia Æthiopica*, on the authority of Father Tellez, a learned Portuguese Jesuit, and from the information of an Abyssinian priest, dates the introduction of Christianity into that part of Africa at a later period. Dr. Kitto, in a note on this text in the last edition of his *Pictorial Bible*, says that the Abyssinians themselves allege that the province of Tigre, the part of their country nearest to that of Merve, was converted by the preaching of this noble chamberlain, although the nation at large did not receive the Gospel till a later day. In accordance with this opinion, Ludolf supposes that the Abyssinians were not converted till the time of Constantine the Great, about A.D. 330. Whichever be the fact, it is certain that the Abyssinians have, ever since that time, continued in the Christian faith and kept the sacramental institutions of Christ, without yielding to the interpolations of the Church of Rome, although severely pressed upon them by all the authority that

one of their own emperors could exert.  Ludolf has
given a full account of these Christian negroes and
their Church.  They retained baptism by water, and
communicated in both kinds, and drove out the Portuguese Jesuits for attempting, by force, to pervert
and corrupt these primitive rites.  These negroes
are a lasting monument of Christianity among the
sons of Ham.

Christianity must have made a rapid progress in
Africa, for we read of a council of African and
Numidian bishops held at Carthage so early as A.D.
215,—a time when our Anglo-Saxon ancestors were
immersed in Pagan darkness, in which they continued
for four centuries.  In A.D. 240 a council of ninety
and nine bishops was held at Lambesa,* an inland
city of Africa, on the confines of Biledulgerid, against
Privatus, Bishop of Lambesa, on a charge of heresy.
The fourth council of Carthage, A.D. 253, consisted

* Dr. Cave's *Scriptorum Ecclesiasticorum Historia Lite-
raria*, 2 vols., folio, 1688, 1698, and Oxford, 2 vols, folio,
1740, 1743.

of sixty-six bishops, and was held* to settle the matter concerning the baptism of infants; and in the eighth council held in that city A.D. 256, there were eighty-seven bishops, and a large representative body of priests, deacons and layman.† In another council at Carthage about A.D. 308,‡ no less than two hundred and seventy bishops of the sect of Donatists§ were present; and in A.D. 396‖ a council of three hundred and ten bishops was held at Baga, an inland city of Africa. These eminent Christian councils were all long before the conversion of the English to Christianity.

Hume, in his essay on National Characters, Mr. Samuel Eswich, M.A., assistant-agent for the island

---

* Dr. Cave's *Scrip. Eccl. Hist. Lit.*

† " Presentes erant preter presbyteros, diaconos, maximamque plebis partem, episcopi lxxxvii.," etc. Ibid. Also Bohun's *Geographical Dictionary*, art. Lambesa.

‡ Ibid.

§ Followers of Donatus, Bishop of Casæ Negræ, in Numidia, in the fourth century.

‖ Dr. Cave's *Scrip. Eccl. Hist. Lit.*

of Barbadoes, who follows Hume's arguments very
closely, and other modern writers, assert, and attempt to prove, that negroes are an inferior race of
men.  What would the facts just cited, of the early
civilization and learning of Africa prove before an
impartial jury, when weighed against the unsupported assertions of such mere advocates?  Aristotle
asserts, in an equally unsupported* argument, "that
men of little genius and great bodily strength *are
destined by Nature to serve,* and those of better
capacity *to command;* and that the natives of Greece
and of some other countries, being *naturally* superior
in genius, have *a natural right* to empire; and that
the rest of mankind, being *naturally* stupid, are
destined by Nature to labour and slavery."  Dr.
Beattie, in his highly popular and admirable *Essay
on Truth,* the first edition of which was published
in 1770, and a splendid one in 1777—the year
when Granville Sharp was attacking " the accursed

* *De Republicâ,* lib. i., cap. 5, 6.

thing,"—thus replies* to these advocates of natural superiority and inferiority of races: "That I may not be thought a blind admirer of antiquity, I would here crave the reader's indulgence for a short digression to put him in mind of an important error in morals, inferred from Aristotle himself. He argues that men of little genius and great bodily strength are by nature destined to serve, and those of better capacity to obey," etc., as before quoted. Dr. Beattie then replies: " This reasoning is now, alas ! of little advantage to Aristotle's countrymen,† who have for many ages been *doomed to that slavery*, which, in his judgment, *Nature had destined them to impose upon others ;* and many nations whom he would *consign to everlasting stupidity*, have shown

---

* *Essay on Truth*, p. 458—464.

† It is now (1853) exactly four centuries since Mahomet II. signed a treaty of peace with the subjugated Greek Emperor, Constantine Drakoses, in the spring of A.D. 1453, making Constantinople the seat of his empire on the 29th of May of that year. After the death of the brave Greek prince, Leandenberg, in 1467, all Greece became vassals to the Turks.

themselves equal in genius to the most exalted of
human kind.  It would have been more worthy of
Aristotle to have inferred man's natural and universal
right to liberty, from that natural and universal
passion with which men desire it.  He wanted,
perhaps, to devise some excuse for servitude; a
practice which, to their eternal reproach, both Greeks
and Romans tolerated even in the days of their
glory.

"Mr. Hume argues nearly in the same manner in
regard to the superiority of white men over black.*
'I am apt to expect,' he says, 'that the negroes,
and in general all the other species of men, (for there
are four or five different kinds,) to be naturally
inferior to the whites.  There *never was* a civilized
nation of any other complexion than white, *nor even
any individual*, eminent either in action or speculation.  *No* ingenious manufacturers among them, *no*
arts, *no* sciences.  There are negro slaves dispersed

---

* *Essay on National Characters.*

all over Europe, of which *none* ever discovered any symptoms of ingenuity.' These assertions are strong; but I know not whether they have anything else to recommend them. For, first, though true, they would not prove the point in question, except it were also proved that the Africans and Americans, even though arts and sciences were introduced among them, would still remain unsusceptible of cultivation. *The inhabitants of Great Britain and France were as savage two thousand years ago, as those of Africa and America are at this day.** To civilize a nation is a work which requires long time to accomplish. *One may as well say of an infant that he can never become a man, as of a nation, now barbarous, that it can never be civilized.* Secondly, of the facts here asserted no man could have sufficient evidence, except from a personal acquaintance with all the negroes that now are, or ever were, upon the face of the earth. Those people write no

---

* A.D. 1770.

histories, and all the reports of all the travellers that ever visited them will not amount to anything like a proof of what is here affirmed. But, thirdly, WE KNOW THAT THESE ASSERTIONS ARE NOT TRUE. The empires of Peru and Mexico could not have been governed, nor the metropolis of the latter have been built after so singular a manner in the middle of a lake, *without men eminent both for action and speculation.* Everybody has heard of the magnificence, good government and ingenuity of the ancient Peruvians. The Africans and Americans are known to have many ingenious arts and manufactures among them, which even Europeans would find it no easy matter to imitate. Sciences, indeed, they have none, because they have no letters; but in oratory, some of them, particularly the Indians of the five nations, are said to be greatly our superiors. It will readily be allowed that the condition of a slave is not favourable to genius of any kind; yet the negro slaves dispersed over Europe have, contrary to Mr. Hume's assertion, often discovered symptoms of ingenuity notwithstanding* their unhappy circumstances.  They

---

* The case of that singular negro, Ignatius Sancho, is a complete exemplification of this argument.  He was born at sea in 1729, on board a slave ship in its passage from Africa to the Spanish Main; and on his arrival at Carthagena received from his owner the name of Ignatius at the baptismal font.  Accompanying his master to England, he was given by him, as he would a monkey or a parrot, to three maiden sisters who resided in Greenwich.  These ladies employed him in menial offices; and bestowed on him his second name—Sancho, "in allusion," says Jekyll in his life of this extraordinary man, "to the doughty squire of Don Quixote."  He fortunately attracted the notice of the Duke of Montagu, who rescued him from a harsh servitude, took him into his own service, and continued his steady friend through life.  On the death of the Duchess, who survived her husband, Sancho with an annuity of £30, bequeathed to him by that benevolent lady, became for the first time his own master; and falling into irregular habits, his annuity was soon dissipated.  As a means of support he tried the stage, and appeared as Othello and Oronoco.  In this attempt he was unsuccessful, having few requisites for the parts assumed except his colour, good sense, and a correct reading of his author.  Soon after this failure he married a young Creole possessed of a little property, by which, with the continued friendship of the family of his noble patron and his literary ability, he was restored to comfort and respectability.  This remarkable man was the author of some excellent letters, that were collected and published after his death, which occurred at Christmas

become excellent handicraft's men* and practical musicians, and learn indeed *everything* their masters are at pains to teach them—perfidy and debauchery not excepted.

"That a negro slave who can neither read nor write, nor speak any European language ; who is not permitted to do anything but what his master commands, and who has not a single friend on earth, and is universally considered and treated as if he were of a species inferior to the human ;—that such a creature should so distinguish himself among Europeans, as to be talked of through the world for a man of genius, is surely no reasonable expectation. To suppose him to be of an inferior species because

---

1780. They were highly commended by many of the great literary characters of the day, particularly by Dr. Johnson, Garrick and Sterne. He also wrote some miscellaneous poetry and a tract on music. So much for the theory of Aristotle and the assertions of Hume.

* For proofs of this, see hereafter the manufactures and other articles of ingenuity by negroes, produced by Mr. Clarkson before the Parliamentary and other committees.

he does not thus distinguish himself, is just as rational as to suppose any private European must be of an inferior species because he has not raised himself to the condition of royalty.

" Had the Europeans," continues Dr. Beattie, "been destitute of the arts of writing* and working in iron, they might have remained to this day as barbarous as the natives of Africa and America. Nor is the invention of these arts to be ascribed to our superior capacity. The genius of the inventor is not always to be estimated according to the importance of the invention. Gunpowder and the mariner's compass have produced wonderful revolutions in human affairs, and yet were *accidental discoveries*. Such, probably, were the first essays in writing and working in metal. Suppose them to have been the effects of contrivance, they were at least contrived by a few individuals; and if they

---

* These arts and many others are of very remote antiquity, and of Asiatic origin. See Moses, Homer, Herodotus, etc.

required a superiority of understanding or of species in the inventors, those inventors and their descendants are the only persons who can lay claim to the honour of that superiority.

" That every practice and sentiment is barbarous that is not according to the usages of modern Europe, seems to be a fundamental maxim with many of our critics and philosophers. Their remarks often put us in mind of the fable of the man and the lion. If negroes and Indians were disposed to recriminate; if a Lucian or a Voltaire from the coast of Guinea or from the five nations were to pay us a visit; what a picture of European manners might he present to his countrymen on his return! Nor would caricature or exaggeration be necessary to render it hideous. A plain historical account of some of our most fashionable duellists, gamblers and adulterers, to name no others, would exhibit specimens of brutish barbarity and sottish infatuation as might vie with any that ever appeared in Kamschatka, California or the land of Hottentots.

" It is easy to see with what views some modern authors throw out these hints to prove the natural inferiority of negroes. But let every friend to humanity pray that they may be disappointed. Britons are famous for generosity ; a virtue in which it is easy for them to excel both the Romans and the Greeks. Let it never be said that *slavery* is countenanced by the bravest and most generous people upon earth,—by a people who are animated by that heroic passion, *the love of liberty*, beyond all nations—ancient or modern ; and the fame of whose toilsome but unwearied perseverance, in vindicating at the expense of life and fortune the sacred rights of mankind, will strike terror into the hearts of sycophants and tyrants, and excite the admiration and the gratitude of all good men to the latest posterity."

The great question whether slavery could exist in Great Britain, which was so triumphantly carried in the negative by Mr. Granville Sharp, in the celebrated case of *Stewart and Somerset*, in the Court of King's Bench, in the teeth of Lords Hardwicke's and Talbot's affirmative decisions, belongs in its generality and details to the history of the abolition of the slave trade and slavery ; but a brief sketch of which is necessary to a clear understanding of the following narrative.

In the year 1769, Mr. Sharp, who was then a barrister of distinguished biblical, classical and forensic learning, published a tract called *A Representation of the Injustice and dangerous Tendency of tolerating Slavery, or of admitting the least Claim of Private Property in the persons of Men in England: being an Answer to an Opinion given in the year 1729 by the Attorney-General and Solicitor-General concerning the case of Slaves in Great Britain.* Mr. Sharp relates in another work,* that he had certain proofs of no less than three married women being violently torn away from their lawful husbands, *even in London,* by the order of their pretended proprietors. He gives another remarkable instance

---

* *The Just Limitation of Slavery in the Laws of God.* 8vo. London, 1776. p. 34.

which came within his own knowledge, which was the advertising a reward, in the *London Gazette* of June 1, 1772, for the apprehension of " *an East India black boy, about* 14 *years of age, named Bob or Pompey* ;" his identity was further distinguished by " *having round his neck a brass collar* with a direction upon it to a house in Charlotte Street, Bloomsbury Square." " Thus," says the philanthropic lawyer, " the black Indian Pompey was manifestly treated with as little ceremony as a black namesake of the dog kind could be." Mr. Sharp enquired after the author of this unlawful and shameful advertisement; and found that he was a merchant in the heart of the city of London.

In addition to an overwhelming confutation of the doctrine then held by the advocates of African slavery, of its practice and countenance by the Mosaic Law, of its being in fact a Divine command, and an obedience to the curse of Noah on his son Canaan and his posterity, who were to be servants of servants to their brethren,—and that the Africans were these accursed descendants;* this learned and profound lawyer, in direct opposition to the *dicta* of Lords Hardwicke and Talbot, proved that an action of trover could not, by the laws of England, lie for the recovery of a slave, and that no man could lawfully be prosecuted for protecting a negro, or any other slave whatever, who had escaped from his master; because that would be punishing a man for doing his indispensable duty, according to the laws of God; and " if any law, custom, or precedent," said this acute and liberal lawyer, "should be alleged to the contrary, it must necessarily be rejected as *null* and *void;* because it is a maxim of the common

---

* The Africans are not descended from Canaan, if we except the Carthagenians, a colony from the sea coast of the Canaanites, who were a *free* people, and at one time rivals in power with the Romans. The Africans are principally descended from *Cush, Mizraim* and *Phut,* the three other sons of Ham. There is still a kingdom in Africa called *Foat,* which Bryant thinks is the country upon the river Gambia, which is at this day, according to M. Bluet, in his *History of Juba ben Sarmon,* called Phuta, after Phut, the third son of Ham.

law of England* that "*the inferior law must give place to the superior,—man's laws to God's laws.*" And the learned author of *The Doctor and the Student*, asserts,† that even statute law ought to be accounted null and void if it is set forth contrary to the laws of God." "Etiam si aliquod statutum esse editum, contra eos nullius vigoris in legibus Anglice censeri debet," etc.

Blackstone affirms,‡ that "the *natural liberty of mankind* consists, properly, in a power of acting as one thinks fit, without any restraint or control, unless by the law of Nature; being *a right inherent in us by birth, and one of the gifts of God to man* at his creation, when he endued him with the faculty of free will." In another place§ he says: "An Act of Parliament is controllable by the laws of God and Nature; and, in its consequences, may be

---

* *The Grounds and Maxims of English Law.* By Attorney-General Noy. p. 19.

† Chapter vi.        ‡ *Comment.*, i., 125.

§ Ibid., 91; and Bacon's *Abridg.*, iv., 639.

rendered void for absurdity, or a manifest contradiction to common reason." Sir John Strange also affirms,* "Christianity is a part of the law of England."

Thomas Blackwell, author of the excellent *Enquiry into the Life and Writings of Homer*, in his *Memoirs† of the Court of Augustus* furnished Mr. Sharp with the following glowing definition, or rather description, of liberty, which he used as a powerful auxiliary against the laws of Lords Hardwicke and Talbot. "Liberty, the most manly and exalting of the gifts of heaven, consists in a free and generous exercise of all the human faculties, as far as they are compatible with the good of society to which we belong; and the most delicious part of the enjoyment of the inestimable blessing lies in a consciousness that we are *free*. This happy persuasion, when it meets with a noble nature, raises the soul and rectifies the heart. It gives dignity to the counte-

---

* Strange's Reports, 1113.

† London, 3 vols. 4to. 1753, 1755 and 1764.

nance, and animates every word and gesture. It elevates the mind above the little arts of deceit, makes it benevolent, open, ingenuous and just, and adds a new relish to every better sentiment of humanity." Having shewn this side of the medal, he points to the reverse, which he takes from his favourite Homer, who says, "Man is bereaved of half his virtues, the day when he is cast into bondage." Our Addison, who was both a statesman and a poet, and moreover a Christian, makes his hero* exclaim,

"A day, an hour, of virtuous liberty
Is worth a whole eternity in bondage."

The cause which led Mr. Sharp to this consideration of the divine and human laws relating to slavery was as follows.† A poor and friendless negro, named James Somersett, having been brought to England by his master, was turned out by him

---

* Addison's *Cato*.

† See Nichols's *Lit. Anec.*,—Life of Granville Sharp, by Hoare, etc. *The Just Limitation of Slavery*, p. 15.

during a fit of sickness, which he felt indisposed to go to the expense of curing, into the streets of the metropolis, to die or recover, as best he might. Mr. Sharp acted the part of the good Samaritan to this poor, degraded, afflicted African stranger, whom he restored to health and to the ability of supporting himself by his own exertions. With unparalleled baseness, this man, whose name Mr. Sharp charitably concealed, as he warred not with the individual but with the crime, brought and tried this action. The matter being now a fact in history, such concealment is unnecessary, and the names of the owner, *Charles Stewart, Esq.*, and of the master of the ship, *Knowles*, who sent the poor fellow adrift by command of his owner, have obtained an unenviable notoriety in the annals of oppression and cruelty.

In the year 1729, Sir Philip Yorke, Attorney-General, and Mr. Talbot, Solicitor-General, pledged themselves to the British planters, in opinions upon a case submitted to them, for the legal consequences of bringing negro slaves into this kingdom, or their being baptized; which opinion was repeated and recognized by the former eminent oracle of the law, when Earl of Hardwicke, and sitting as Lord High Chancellor, on the 19th of October, 1749, to the following effect. He said that " *trover would lay for a negro slave:* that a notion prevailed, that if a slave came into England, or became a Christian, he therefore became emancipated; but there was no foundation in law for such a notion. When he and Lord Talbot," he said, "were Attorney and Solicitor-General, this notion of a slave becoming free by being baptized prevailed so strongly, that the planters industriously prevented their becoming Christians; upon which their opinion was taken. Upon the best consideration of the case, they were both clearly of opinion that *a slave did not in the least alter his situation or state towards his master or owner, either by being christened, or by coming to England.* That although the statute of Charles II. had abolished homage tenure, so far that no man could be a *villein regardant;* yet if he would acknowledge himself a *villein* engrossed, in any court of record, he knew of no way by which he could be entitled to his freedom without the consent of his master." Thus stood Lord Hardwicke's judgment.

In spite of this eminent decision, so thoroughly was Mr. Sharp convinced of its inconsistency with the laws of GOD, of nature and of this realm, and that trover could not lye,* that he counselled and conducted the cases of *Knowles* and *Somersett,* and *Somersett* and *Stewart,* after having published a tract† in which he successfully refuted the opinions of Lords Hardwicke and Talbot, and procured their reversal by the Court of King's Bench in favour of the negro Somersett.

On Monday, the 22nd of June, in Trinity Term, 1772, the Court of King's Bench, proceeded to give judgment in the case of *James Somersett,* a negro,

---

* Vide *Anteà*, p. 31.

† *A Representation of the Injustice and Dangerous Tendency of tolerating Slavery in England.* London, 1769.

against his former master, *Charles Stewart,* Esq., upon the return of the *Habeas Corpus.*

Lord Mansfield, Chief Justice, pronounced the unanimous sentiments and judgment of the whole Bench. His lordship first stated the return, and then spoke to the following purport, which is taken from the second edition of a tract\* published in 1773. "We pay due attention to the opinions of Sir Philip Yorke and Mr. Talbot in the year 1729;" which his lordship quoted at length, without the least comment, its purport being that the master might legally compel his slave to return to the plantation; and added, "We feel the force of the inconveniences and consequences that will follow the decision of this question. Yet all of us are so clearly of one opinion upon the *only* question before us, that

---

\* *Considerations on the Negro Cause, so called, addressed to the Right Hon. Lord Mansfield, Lord Chief Justice of the Court of King's Bench.* By Samuel Estwick, A.M., Assistant-Agent for the Island of Barbadoes. Second Edition. London, 1773.

we think we ought to give judgment without adjourning the matter to be argued before all the judges, as is usual in the *Habeas Corpus;* and as we at first intimated an intention of doing in this case. The only question then is, *Is the cause returned sufficient for the remanding him? If not, he must be discharged.* The cause returned is, that the slave absented himself, and departed from his master's service, and refused to return and serve him during his stay in England. Whereupon, by his master's orders, he was put on board the ship by force, and there detained in secure custody, to be carried out of the kingdom and sold. So high an act of dominion must derive its authority, *if any such it has,* from the law of the kingdom *wherein* it was executed. A foreigner cannot be imprisoned *here* on the authority of any law existing in his own country. The power of a master over his servant is different in all countries, more or less limited or extensive. The exercise of it, therefore, must always be regulated by the laws of the place where exercised."

" The state of slavery is of such a nature, that it is incapable of being now introduced by courts of justice upon mere reasoning, or by inferences drawn from any principles, natural or political. It must take its rise from *positive law;* the origin of it can in no country or age be traced back to any other source. Immemorial usage preserves the memory of *positive law* long after all traces of the occasion, reason, authority and time of its introduction are lost; and in a case so odious as the condition of slaves, it must be taken strictly. Tracing the subject to natural principles, the claim of slavery can never be supported. The power claimed by this return was never in use *here,* nor acknowledged by the law. No master ever was allowed here to take a slave by force to be sold abroad because he had deserted from his service, or for any other reason whatever. We cannot say that the cause set forth by this return is allowed or approved of by the laws of this kingdom; and therefore *the man must be discharged.*"

This eminent luminary of British jurisprudence,

by this important judgment, demolished in a few short sentences the empty sophistry and illegal opinion of Attorney-General Yorke and Solicitor-General Talbot, that slave owners may legally compel their slaves to return from England and freedom, to their plantations and slavery. This opinion, be it remarked, like all such opinions of counsel, was founded on a case drawn up by the advocates of slavery, and was not of authority like a decision or judgment of a court of law.

This judgment proved the correctness of Mr. Sharp's legal knowledge, and triumphantly recorded the seldom-doubted fact of the freedom of the British soil. It decided that *Stewart's* claim to property in *Somersett*, and *Knowles's* trover to recover possession of him, were contrary to the three principal foundations of English law—nature, usage and statute, or the written law ; which last includes maxims and statutes. These were the reasons for the judgment, and "consequently," says Mr. Sharp,* "the court

---

* In his " Remarks on that judgment," p. 74.

was obliged by the common law, which always favours* liberty, to discharge the man from the unnatural and unprecedented claims of his master." This was accordingly done; James Somersett was emancipated, and the fact proclaimed that the British soil gave freedom to the slave.

This triumph was shortly followed by two others founded on this great precedent. One in the Prerogative Court, Doctors' Commons, the 12th of May, 1773, in the case of *Cay and Crighton*, in which a person who died in 1769 left, among other property, a negro servant named Crighton. The executor was called upon by Cay to give an inventory of the deceased's *goods* and *chattels*, which he did, but omitted to specify the negro. This omission was made a ground of exception to the inventory, as being therefore imperfect. Upon argument it was

---

* "Law favoureth life, *liberty* and power." "Law regardeth the person above his possessions." "Life and *liberty* most," etc.—*Principia Legis et Equit.*, p. 56. "Libertas est res inestimabilis."—Jenk. *Cent.*, 52.

said by the counsel, on behalf of Crighton, that by a very recent case in the King's Bench, of *Knowles and Somersett, negroes were declared to be free in England ;* and consequently could not be subjects of *property,* or be considered as any part of a personal estate.

It was answered that the case mentioned was determined only in 1772, whereas the testator died in 1769, at which time negroes were in some respects considered as property ; and that he ought, therefore, to be included in the account.

The judge, Dr. Hay, said that this court had no right to try any question relating to freedom and slavery. But as negroes had been declared free by the court which had the proper jurisdiction, that determination referred as well to the preceding time as the present. He therefore directed that the article in which the negro was mentioned to be struck out of the exceptive allegation.

The other was the case of *Rogers,* alias *Rigges,* against *Jones,* in the High Court of Admiralty,

before Sir George Hay, Knt., LL.D., etc., the 29th
of June, 1776; Drs. Wynne and Bever, with Proctor Torriano, were for *Rogers;* and Drs. Harris and
Calvert, with Proctor Holman, were for *Jones.*

George Rogers, alias Rigges, it appeared, was a
negro about nineteen years of age, who had been a
servant to several gentlemen in England. In the
summer of 1766, being then out of place, he became
acquainted with John Latter and John Lessins, who
contracted with Arthur *Jones* for the sale of him.
An assignment was accordingly drawn for that purpose, and signed by John Latter, by which *Rogers*
was transferred to Messrs. Mason and Jones, as a
slave, for the sum of twelve guineas.

Some time in August, 1776, after the beforementioned sale, *Rogers* was taken, under some false
pretences, on board the ship Britannia, lying at
Deptford, of which Mason and Jones were owners.
He was there detained against his will, and that he
might not escape, was carried down, by order of
the chief mate, into the sail room, and the gratings

were put over him. He was kept in this confinement till the ship sailed, when he was released. But not being entered in the ship's books as a seaman, nor having any specific offices or wages assigned to him, he was set about the general duties of the ship till he was appointed assistant to the cook, acting sometimes as principal cook during the voyage. The ship sailed first to the coast of Africa, in the slave trade, and thence to Porto Rico, where he was offered for sale by the captain of the Britannia as a prime slave. But Rogers having found an opportunity of relating his story to the Spanish merchants, they refused to buy him. He therefore returned with the ship, in which he still acted as the cook's mate, and on their arrival in the port of London in May, 1768, when the other seamen were paid and discharged, he was detained on board against his will.

In this situation he continued for some time, till he contrived to make his escape, when by the advice and assistance of some friends he went to Doctors'

Commons, and applied to Mr. Falkner, a proctor, to assist him in recovering his wages, or some remuneration for his labours. Mr. Falkner, therefore, wrote to Arthur Jones, one of the owners, for payment; and Rogers being appointed to meet Jones at the proctor's office, waited at a public house in the neighbourhood till he should be sent for. Whilst he was thus waiting, Jones, Seffins and another man entered the house, forced Rogers into a coach, carried him away, and forced him on board another ship, where he was chained to the main-mast. In this horrible situation he was kept, till he was released by the Deputy-Marshal of the High Court of Admiralty, with the assistance of Mr. Shea, one of his former masters, and some other friends, who had obtained a warrant to release him from his confinement.

Several reasons prevented him from applying for a redress of these grievances until the beginning of the year 1774, when Mr. Torriano was employed to commence an action against Jones, as one of the owners, for the purpose of recovering the wages or remuneration for his services. After the usual preliminary measures the cause was brought on for hearing the 29th of June, 1776, when the before-mentioned facts having been clearly proved, the principal question was, " *How far the plea of slavery set up by the defendant could be admitted in bar of the wages ?*"

It was insisted on by the counsel for *Rogers* that the kind of slavery there spoken of never had any existence under the laws of England, and in support of his proposition referred to the well-known case of *Knowles and Somersett* before Lord Chief-Justice Mansfield, and likewise to the last-mentioned one in the Prerogative Court of *Cay and Crighton.*

The counsel for the defendant argued that until the case of *Somersett,* the law of England admitted slavery; and, in support of this argument, quoted the authority of Lord Chief-Justice Hale, and, in particular, the opinions of the Lords Hardwicke and Talbot.

The decree of the court, which in full must take its place in the history of the abolition of the slave trade, being too long for this preliminary sketch of one of its great heroes, was to the following effect.

The learned judge, Sir George Hay, said there were two principal points in the cause, namely, *first*, whether such service was proved as to entitle the plaintiff to the wages demanded; and *secondly*, whether the plea of slavery was a sufficient bar to the claim.

With regard to the *first*, it appeared that the Plaintiff had served on board the ship either in the capacity of assistant cook or as cook during the greatest part of the voyage, and was entitled to some recompence for his services. But not having been entered in the ship's book as a mariner, nor having any stipulated wages assigned to him, it being probable that the owners meant to sell him in the West Indies, he cannot be allowed any precise sum under the name of *wages;* but as he performed the duty to which he was assigned without any objection to his behaviour in it, the maritime law clearly gives him a *quantum meruit*. The cook's wages appear to have been £1 5*s*. 6*d*. per month, which is more than *Rogers* most probably could fairly deserve. But upon inspecting the mariner's contract, it appears there were several negro boys in the same ship in the quality of apprentices who were allowed from 10*s*. to 17*s*. 6*d*. per month. He therefore was of opinion that *Rogers* might fairly deserve 15*s*. per month, which he decreed him from the time of his being first carried on board.

With regard to the *second* point, it had been urged, said the judge, that *the plaintiff was a slave*, and consequently was not entitled to any reward for his services. The practice of buying and selling slaves, he emphatically remarked, was certainly very common in England *before the case of Somerset ; but however it might have been the law of the Royal Exchange, it never was the law of England.*

The opinions of Lord Hardwicke, when Attorney General, and Lord Talbot, when Solicitor-General, had been quoted in support of this practice, and had formerly given too much countenance to it, although they seemed *originally* to have been applied *only* to the difference created by baptism. But by the late *determination of one of the ablest judges that ever presided in this kingdom, these opinions have been held to be mistaken and unsound;* and there can be no further doubt that *the claim of slavery is not maintainable by the law of England.*

The law, therefore, said the learned judge, was the same before the time of those *"opinions"* as since, and consequently refers to all sales of this nature, which are illegal, and therefore the pretended sale, in the present case, in 1776 was an absolute nullity; and when the allegation which stated the sale was admitted on behalf of the owners, had *Rogers* appeared under protest upon this point of law, it would not have been received in bar of the plea. The owners have acted upon a mistaken notion of their right; but as the claim of slavery is clearly against the laws of this country, and as it appeared that *Rogers* had always acted in some useful capacity

E

during the whole time he was on board, he, the judge, considered him entitled to a *quantum meruit* for his services.

Such were the important results which arose from Mr. Sharp's wise, energetic, philanthropic and legal conduct in this celebrated case; and such was the literary and legal state of the question when the kindred spirit of the Vice-Chancellor of Cambridge propounded his no less important *thesis* to the young and animated minds of the aspiring undergraduates of his university. But, before returning to the immediate subject of this precursory memoir, we will mention an incident which occurred, and which proves that there is no romance more romantic than truth, and which was developed to the world by this very transaction of Granville Sharp.

In the *General Evening Post* of the 13th of June, 1772, appeared a letter from a correspondent, which stated, that the great cause then pending* between

---

* Lord Mansfield's luminous judgment was delivered on the 22nd of that month.

Mr. Stewart and the negro Somersett being the principal topic of general conversation, he forwarded to the editor of that widely circulated newspaper, a copy of a letter from a gentleman in Maryland to his friend in Philadelphia, from which the following passages and narrative are extracted.

" I am so happy as to think as you do concerning the trading in man, or keeping him as a slave. The custom is wicked and iniquitous, neither consistent with reason nor with the laws of GOD or man." The writer, after pitying their forlorn state, particularly those who had been forced from the land of their birth, says, that although a slave-owner, he never *bought* more than two in his life. One of these purchases proved to be the son of an African Prince, and was a most comely youth. His new owner, perceiving his good natural abilities, sent him to school, and used him like a free man during his stay with him. The Directors of the African Company having heard of the circumstance offered a large reward for him, but his humane mas-

ter by a public act, as was necessary, presented him
with his freedom, sent him to London, and gave him
an order to receive the reward offered by the Company. From that place, he remitted in the following
year to his humane master the sum for which he had
bought him, and sundry rich goods to the amount of
£300 more, accompanied by a letter in his native
language.

The other purchased slave, alluded to by this
most Christian planter, was an unhappy lad, kidnapped from his *free* parents at the capture of Gua-
daloupe. " During his stay with me," writes this
excellent man, whose name I regret has escaped my
research, " he decayed and pined so much, and expressed so sensible a sorrow for his cruel separation
from his parents, relations and countrymen, that,
actuated by the unerring good Providence which
directs us in all our good deeds, I likewise set this
poor creature free, and sent him to his native place.

" Providence," he gratefully adds, " would not
excuse my being further rewarded for performing

this my duty as a Christian. The truly honest father has made me presents to the amount of £50 sterling, with directions to draw upon him for the full cost of the poor youth, which I do never intend." Well does our great bard say of mercy, that,

"It droppeth, as the gentle rain from Heav'n,
Upon the place beneath. It is twice bless'd;
It blesses him that gives and him that takes."

This exemplary Maryland planter informs his Pennsylvanian friend, that he wrote to convince him that the natives of Africa were not such senseless, brutish creatures, as thoughtless authors represent them to be. He asserts from his own practical knowledge and experience, that "they are, undoubtedly, capable of receiving instruction, and far outdo Christians in many commendable virtues.

"Poor creatures," he pathetically exclaims, "*their greatest unhappiness is being acquainted with Christians.*" The benevolent writer of this epistle to the Philadelphians, evidently means in this last sentence by 'Christians,' white men—the gods of Mr. Hume, as a class ; men who so call themselves, but have none of the great qualities of the Christian—mercy and charity—in them.

The following translation of the letter referred to, as written from the Negro Prince to his before-mentioned benevolent owner, was made by the Rev. Dr. Desaguillers,* at Cambridge, in 1743, from the original.

"From the Great City,

"Third moon after my release.

"Oh, my kind merciful master, my good white brother,—too good, a very good son of a very good woman and of a very good old man,—created good old people by the GREAT SPIRIT who made my coun-

---

* John Theophilus Desaguillers, LL.D., F.R.S., etc., was the son of a Protestant clergyman of Rochelle, who was driven from his home by the revocation of the edict of Nantes, and took refuge in England with his infant son, then two years old. The latter was educated at Oxford, was ordained and obtained preferment in the Church of England. He is well known as a mathematician, natural philosopher and scholar. He died in 1749, in the 67th year of his age.

try, thy poor—I should say, *heretofore* poor—most grateful black prisoner, now rendered rich by thy goodness and mercy, is now most dead, most drunk, most mad with joy! Why is he so? Because he is going to his good warm country,* to his good old mother, to his good old father, to his little sister and his brother. In my good warm country all things are good except the white people who live there, and come in flying houses to take away poor black prisoners from their mothers, their fathers, their sisters and their brothers, to kill them with hunger and filth in the cellars of their flying houses, where-in, if they do not die fast enough (and poor prisoners talk for bread and water, and want to feel the winds,

---

* Dr. Chalmers, in his *History of the Diseases of South Carolina* (Vol. I., p. 18), states that in South Carolina, in the year 1752, during the months of June and July, the weather was hotter than had ever been remembered in that country. The thermometer stood in the shade at 115°, and the heat out of doors was too great for his instrument to measure; yet his *negroes* informed him, that *they* preferred that sort of weather to the winter's cold.

and to see the GREAT SPIRIT—to complain to Him to tell Him all, or to see the trees of his good warm country once more for the last time), the king* of the white people orders the officer called *Jack* to kill many of the black prisoners with whips, with ropes, knives, axes and salt. The governor of thy flying house has been to show that which is to carry me and him to my warm country : I am glad, very glad indeed ! He goes there with wine. Should he be sick, and white men seldom escape being so there, because of thee, my kind merciful master and good white brother! and because he has been good to me, and is a very good white man too, I will nurse him myself; my mother, my father, my little sister and my brother, shall be his brother, his mother, his father and his sister too. He shall have one large heap of elephants' teeth and gold for thee, my kind merciful master and kind brother; and one for himself also, but smaller. He, at present, is my

* Probably he means the captain of the slave ship.

father : I eat at his house, and lie too upon the bed thou presented to me. His woman is my mother, and kindly nurses me, being very sick of the sea and of fire made of black stones. I have received a great quantity of gold besides what thou didst present me with, by means of thy hand-writing to the people who are to send me to my country ; some part whereof I have given to the governor of thy swimming house to be sent to thee. Had I an houseful, should send the whole with equal pleasure. However, thou shalt see hereafter that black people are not beasts, and do know how to be grateful. After thou, my kind merciful master and good white brother, left me in thy swimming house, we—thy white people, and we—thy grateful black prisoners, were, by the GREAT SPIRIT, who was angry with us, sent by the wind into an immense great river, where we had like to have been drowned, and where we could see neither sun nor moon for six days and nights. I was dying during one whole moon ; the governor was my father, and gave me those good things thou presented me with, on my bed. He lodged me in the little room thy carpenter built for me. Thou gave me more clothes than I could carry, yet I was very cold; nothing availed with poor black prisoner, till at last, having the GREAT SPIRIT to send me safe to thy house on shore, I thought I was carried there, where thou,* my good white brother, did use me with wonted goodness, spake to the GREAT SPIRIT and to his Son, that I might keep so during the voyage and afterwards, which they have done for thy sake. They will always do me good, because of thee, my good white brother; therefore, my kind merciful master, do not forget thy poor black prisoner. When thou dost speak to the GREAT SPIRIT and to His Son, I do know He will hear thee; I shall never be sick more, for which I shall be thankful. Pray speak for my good old mother, my good father, my little sister and my brother. I wish they may be healthy to many,

---

* This seems to be the relation of a dream.

very many moons—as many as the hairs on thy head. I love them all much; yet, I think, not so much as I do thee. I could die in my country for thee, could I do thee any kindness. Indeed, the GREAT SPIRIT well knows I mean no lie, shall always speak to Him for thy good. Believe me, my good white brother, thy poor black prisoner is not a liar."

" DGIAGOLA, son of Dgiagola, Prince of Foat,* Africa."

About the time that Dr. Desaguillers translated this singular letter, Shenstone the poet was in London, publishing his *Judgment of Hercules*, his *Schoolmistress* and a volume of his miscellaneous poems. Whether it came across him or not is problematical, but the translator and the poet were of the same University, and probably met at the Royal Society, Lord Lyttelton's, Shenstone's Warwick-

---

* See note (*), page 30.

shire neighbour and patron, or at some other places, where the wits and cognoscenti of the day were wont to congregate. Be this as it may, the subject of negro slavery made a deep impression on the heart of the tender and melodious bard of the *Leasower*, who gave vent to his feelings in the following pensive stanzas.

### AN ELEGY ON THE MISERABLE STATE OF AN AFRICAN SLAVE.

See the poor native quit the Lybian shores,
    Ah not in Love's delightful fetters bound!
No radiant smile his dying peace restores,
    Nor love, nor fame, nor friendship heals his wound.

Let vacant bards display their boasted woes ;
    Shall I the mockery of grief display ?
No, let the muse his piercing pangs disclose,
    Who bleeds and weeps his sum of life away !

On the wild beach in mournful guise he stood,
    Ere the shrill boatswain gave the hated sign :
He dropt a tear unseen into the flood ;
    He stole one secret moment to repine.

Yet the muse listen'd to the plaints he made,—
 Such moving plaints as nature could inspire ;
To me the Muse his tender plea convey'd,
 But smoothed and suited to the sounding lyre.


" Why am I ravish'd from my native strand ?
 What savage race* protects this impious gain ?
Shall foreign plagues infest this teeming land,
 And more than sea-born monsters plough the main ?


" Here the dire locusts' horrid swarms prevail ;
 Here the blue asps with livid poison swell ;
Here the dry dipsa† writhes his sinuous mail ;
 O, can we not here secure from envy dwell ?


" When the grim lion urg'd his cruel chase,
 When the stern panther sought his midnight prey,

---

 \* At that time this " savage race " was *British* ; which it is now, let the *American* President, *Pierce,* answer.

 † A serpent whose bite produces the sensation of unquench-able thirst. Διψα, *sitis, vehemens desiderium.* It is mentioned by Isidorus and Pliny among the ancients, and by our Milton among the moderns :—

  " Scorpion and asp, and amphibrena dire,
   Cerastes horn'd, hydrus and eliops drear,
   And *dipsas.*"

What fate reserv'd me for this Christian race ?*
O, race more polished, more severe than they !

" Ye prowling wolves pursue my latest cries !
Thou hungry tiger, leave thy reeking den !
Ye sandy wastes in rapid eddies rise !
O, tear me from the whips and scorns of *men !*

" Yet in their face superior beauty glows.
Are smiles the mien of rapine and of wrong ?
Yet from their lip the voice of mercy flows,
And ev'n religion dwells upon their tongue.

" Of blissful haunts they tell, and brighter climes,
Where gentle minds convey'd by Death repair,
But stain'd with blood and crimson'd o'er with crimes,
Say, shall they merit what they paint so fair ?

" No, careless, hopeless of those fertile plains,
Rich by our toils, and by our sorrows gay,
They ply our labours and enhance our pains,
And feign those distant regions to repay.

-----

* If what Tillotson says be true, that " we *Christians* have
certainly the best and the holiest, the wisest and most reasonable religion in the world," the poet has put a most biting and
caustic irony into the mouth of his sufferer.

" For *them** our tusky elephant expires ;
    For *them*, we drain the mine's embowell'd gold ;
Where rove the brutal nation's wild desires,
    Our limbs are purchas'd, and our life is sold !

" Yet shores there are, blest shores for us remain,
    And favour'd isles with golden fruitage crown'd,
Where tufted flow'rets paint the verdant plain,
    Where ev'ry breeze shall med'cine ev'ry wound.

" There, the stern tyrant that embitters life
    Shall vainly, suppliant, spread his asking hand ;
*There*, shall we view the billow's raging strife
    Aid the kind breast and waft his boat to land."

      —————

    From the foregoing brief sketch of the period antecedent to the proposition of the Vice-Chancellor's prize, may be gathered the state of the literary and legal opinions of the public upon that important question, which occupied the mind and tongue of every

—————

    * No one could sing with more propriety the " Sic vos non vobis mellificatis apes " of the illustrious Bucolic poet, than the sugar-making Africans of that time and the cotton-planting slaves of the present.

thinking man in Britain, who valued the laws of GOD
and of England above those of the Royal Exchange.
Besides, how remarkably is the hand of GOD visible
in this mighty struggle which removed the " accursed thing" from our land, beginning with the
incipient strife of Granville Sharp in behalf of the
dying negro Somersett, down to the vote of twenty
millions of pounds sterling by the overtaxed people
of England, for the purchase and emancipation of the
slaves, which belonged to an infinitesimal portion of
their fellow-countrymen.   Well might Granville
Sharp emphatically and exultingly exclaim at the
end of one of his tracts on liberty, " SOLI DEO GLO-
RIA ET GRATIA."

With this state of public feeling as to the pitiable
condition of African slaves under British owners,
with the memory of Lord Mansfield's great decision
and luminous judgment for himself and the whole
court of King's Bench, and its double confirmation
as an eternal precedent in English law by that excellent civilian, Sir George Hay, did Vice-Chan-

cellor Peckard propound to his Cantabrigian disciples, " Anne liceat invitos in servitutem dare."

In 1784, the year preceding to this announcement, Mr. Clarkson had gained a prize for the best Latin dissertation; and, therefore, it was expected that he would be a competitor, and obtain one of the prizes in the new contest, or be considered as having lost grade, both in the eyes of the University, in general, and of his own College, in particular. It had occurred, also, that he had been honoured by carrying off the first prize of that year; and, consequently, it was expected, that he should again obtain the first honours on this occasion. The acquisition of the second prize, however honourable in itself, would have been considered by the whole University, as a falling off, and a loss of former reputation. He felt himself, therefore, especially called on to retain his post of honour, and to obtain a higher degree of scholastic fame; and with such exciting feelings he began to prepare himself for the conflict.

In studying the subject proposed, the young

aspirant properly conceived that the proposition, though couched in general terms, pointed indirectly at the African slave-trade, which at that time, from the before-mentioned causes, began to occupy a large share of public attention. He, more particularly, remembered that the Vice-Chancellor* had pronounced his opinions on that subject most emphatically against that inhuman traffic. At any rate, he says in his own account of the transaction, he determined to give that particular construction of the proposition to his thesis. But he lamented his entire ignorance of the subject, and that only a few weeks were allowed for the composition of the work.

He, however, made the best use of his time, and commenced his labours with an earnest determination of doing his best. He procured access to the manuscript papers of a deceased friend, who had been engaged in the trade; and was acquainted, also, with several naval and military officers, who had

---

* In his before-mentioned Sermon.

been in the West Indies and were well informed on the subject of African slavery and of the trade by which it was supported. From these authoritative documents, and the information of these official friends, he gained some authentic practical knowledge. But he still found himself at much loss for the want of substantial materials with which to construct his edifice; and knew not whence to procure them. In this difficulty, he went, as it were, by accident, into the house of a friend, and took up a newspaper that was then lying upon the table, and one of the first things which caught his eye was an advertisement of Benezet's* *Historical Account of*

---

* Anthony Benezet was an American philanthropist of Philadelphia, of a singularly devout and charitable character. He was, in the first instance, placed with a merchant; but finding that commerce excited too worldly a spirit, he apprenticed himself to a cooper, and finally became a schoolmaster, for the remaining part of his life. He was author of *A Caution to Great Britain and her Colonies; in a short representation of the calamitous state of the enslaved Negroes in the British Dominions.* 8vo. 1767. He also wrote the work here noted, *Some historical account of Guinea : with an enquiry into the*

*Guinea.*   He quickly left his friend, and went immediately to London and bought the work; in which
he found almost all the information that he required.
He gathered from its truthful pages a knowledge of
the great names and authorities of Adanson,* Barbot,†

---

*rise and progress of the Slave-trade,* 1772 : with other works
of a similar character.   His extreme simplicity and benevolence
made him the idol of the poor and of the negroes; hundreds
of whom attended his funeral, accompanied by religious persons
of all denominations.   This good man, who contributed so effectually to the honour and glory of humanity, died at Philadelphia in 1784.

 * The celebrated French naturalist, who wrote among other
things, *Histoire Naturelle de Senegal,* 4to., 1757, which colony
he visited in 1748.   He laid before the French East India Company the plan of a colony on the coast of Africa, where all
manner of colonial produce could be raised without enslaving
the negroes.   This scheme was rejected; but in 1760, when the
English became possessed of Senegal, they made him a liberal
offer to communicate his plan, which he patriotically declined
to do.   M. Adanson showed himself in this instance more of a
Frenchman than a cosmopolitan.

 † A French voyager who wrote a description of French and
English America, a translation of which was published in
Churchill's collection of voyages, London, 1732.   He obtained
his information whilst in the service of the French East India
Company.

Smith,* Bosman, Moore and other writers on subjects connected with his enquiry; who, from having been connected with the trade, and from having long resided in Africa and the West Indies, were practically acquainted with the subject, and were reputed as of unquestionable authority. And as the abolition of the slave-trade had not been mooted when they wrote, they cannot be considered as advocating that cause.

Armed thus with these authorities, and provided with information gathered from their abundant stores, Mr. Clarkson began his work. No man, he pathetically says, can imagine the severe trials which the composition of his essay subjected him to. He had expected to find much pleasure in collecting his materials, in arranging and in constructing his *œdicula* to freedom. He anticipated gratification from the invention of his proposed arguments, from the

---

* John Smith, Governor of Virginia and Admiral of New England. He wrote a *History of Virginia, New England, and the Summer Isles.* Folio. 1624.

arrangement of his facts, from the skill to be displayed in the proper connections, from the proofs he should give by induction of the unlawfulness of making persons slaves against their will, and from the laudable aspirations, so natural in a youthful heart, that of being engaged in an innocent contest for literary honours from his *alma mater*.

But all these anticipations of delight were damped by the horrible and astounding facts that presented themselves continually to his view. It was a continued succession of perpetual woe and misery, and nought but gloomy scenes of mental agony and bodily anguish were before him from early morn to dusky night. By day he was wretched; at night he could take but little rest, sometimes not closing his weary eyes for very grief. Chains, whips, fetters, branding-irons, collars as if for wild beasts, blood, gashes, sobs, convulsions, shrieks, as described in the terrific narratives he had consulted, appeared, like frightful realities, in his dreams of the night and mental visions of the day.

At length it became less an object of ambition, as a literary contest for academic honours, than the production of a work that might be of use to the suffering Africans, and a call upon his country to shake off " the accursed thing," which is twice cursed, cursing both the persecutor and the persecuted ; for

> " Heav'n, whose darling attribute we find,
> Is boundless grace, and mercy to mankind,
> *Abhors the cruel.*"                *Dryden.*

With this additional object perpetually in his mind, he regularly, after having read the harrowing accounts in Benezet's faithful pages, slept with a light in his chamber, that he might rise from his couch and note down such thoughts as arose in his mind during the still and solemn hours of night. This practice arose from a fixed determination of putting forth his utmost strength, not merely for university honours, but for the honour of universal human nature ; and that no auxiliary, however

small, should be lost to the argumentative portion
of his thesis.

Having, at length, finished his painful task, he
transmitted his dissertation to the Vice-Chancellor;
and, shortly afterwards, found himself honoured, as
in the previous year, by the award of the first prize.
Thus was the first spark elicited in Clarkson's mind,
which kindled a fire in the whole Christian part of
the English nation; and excited the people throughout the length and breadth of the British Isles,* in
a generous endeavour to alleviate the sufferings and
redress the wrongs of their African brethren; and
thus was the quiet under-graduate of Cambridge
instantaneously converted from a youthful aspirant
for academic bays into

> " The champion of an injured race,
> Among the great and good."
>
> *Bernard Barton.*

As it was the custom in the University of Cam-

---

* Ireland nobly backed the philanthropic cause. See Sir
John Newport's Speech in the House of Commons, June 10,
1806.

bridge for the author of these laureated dissertations to read them in the Senate House, before the assembled University, shortly after the adjudication of the honours, Mr. Clarkson was recalled to Cambridge for that purpose. He returned to his College and performed his academic duty; but on his journey to London, which he performed on horseback, the subject of his recent lucubrations, which had so painfully occupied his mind by night and day, when in his desire to excel he followed the precept of the Roman lyrist,

"Nocturnà versate manu, versate diurnà."

*Hor.*

so completely engrossed his thoughts, and preyed with such frightful energy upon his mind, that he could think of nothing else. He became, as he himself records in his narrative, at times very seriously affected whilst upon the road. He occasionally stopped his horse, dismounted, and proceeded slowly and thoughtfully on foot; frequently endeavouring to persuade himself that the contents of his dissertation could not, by any possibility, be true. The more, however, that he reflected upon the barbarous facts, which he found recorded with such testimonies to their truthfulness in the authorities he had quoted, the more he believed their frightful statements to be true. Approaching the village of Wade's Mill, in Hertfordshire, he sat down in a disconsolate mood upon the grass by the road-side, and held his horse by the bridle. Whilst seated upon this grassy spot, which is as deserving of commemoration, as Whittington's stone on Highgate Hill, the happy thought flashed into his mind, that if the horrifying contents of his academic exercitation were true, the time had come when some person should come forward and put an end to such demoniacal atrocities.

In this state of mental perturbation, the young *alumnus laureatus* reached his home more sad than even had he lost the prize. This overwhelming impression, from which such great results have flowed, occurred, it may be well to mention here, for the sake of historical accuracy, in the summer of the year 1785.

In the course of the autumn of that year, the incipient champion of the abolition of the traffic in human flesh and blood, body and soul, unable to shake off his melancholy feelings, resolved to devote himself to the pious task. He walked frequently in the woods, contiguous to his home, that he might contemplate the all-engrossing subject in silence and in solitude; and found relief for his agitated feelings.

In these umbrageous solitudes, communing in the spirit with himself, the question still recurred to his mind, "Can these things be true?" Still the answer followed as instantaneously as the thunder follows the lightning, "They are—they must be: the testimony is too powerful for doubt." The same results always followed these solitary conferences, and he still resolved that it was necessary that some one should interfere to put an end to the bloody traffic. In such moods, he began to envy those persons of commanding influence in society, who had seats in Parliament, and who had abilities, wealth, connections and power to contend with the might of our colonies, which gained their riches by rapine, blood and murder.

Many difficulties arose before Clarkson could even begin his sacred work.  It struck him, among many other objections, that a young man of only four and twenty years of age, placed, like him, in a very small circle, could not be possessed of that mature judgment, discretion and knowledge of mankind, manners and of things in general, and also was unqualified either to propose or to conduct a measure of such magnitude and importance.  With whom, then, could he unite himself in such a work ?  He considered also that it would be difficult to persuade men of the world to think of the subject as he did ; he feared being treated as a visionary fanatic ; and, even, should he receive encouragement, the task might appear like some of the poetic labours of Hercules, and that even the sanity of his understanding might be suspected.

In musing upon the numerous ramifications of his all-absorbing subject, he hit upon one practicable method, within his own power, of commencing the attack upon this enemy of mankind. This was, to translate his Latin thesis into English, and to publish it, with notes and many necessary additions. By this measure he expected to discover in what manner the public would receive its awful disclosures, and how far it would encourage his proposition for their abolition. He, therefore, determined to take this preliminary step, and in the middle of the gloomy month of November, 1785, he began his melancholy task.

By the middle of January, 1786, he had accomplished half of his work, although he had made great additions to it. His next step was to engage with a bookseller to print and publish it when finished. For this purpose, he called on Mr. Cadell, in the Strand, who was then a well-known bookseller and extensive publisher, and consulted him about his proposed publication. This respectable

publisher advised him, that as the University of
Cambridge had honoured the original dissertation
with its highest prize, that circumstance alone would
ensure a considerable circulation among persons of
taste. Mr. Clarkson was not, however, as he confesses, quite satisfied with this opinion, for he wished
his work to find its way among useful and practicable people; and among such persons as would
think and act with him. He, accordingly, left Mr.
Cadell, with thanks for his advice, but determined
in his own mind to call upon a friend who resided
in the City. In passing the Royal Exchange, he
met Mr. Joseph Hancock, one of the religious
Society of Friends, with whose family his own had
been long united in friendship. This gentleman
asked why he had not published his prize essay?
Clarkson asked him, in return, what made him
think of it, or of its subject? His friend replied,
that his own particular Society, a religious body,
had taken it up as a religious question; and that
many individuals among them were desirous of see-

ing him thereon. Among other persons of his Society, he mentioned, in particular, Mr. James Phillips,
of George Yard, Lombard Street, bookseller, and
Mr. William Dillwyn, of Walthamstow, as being
thus desirous. Mr. Clarkson requested an introduction to these friends, and in a few minutes they were
with Mr. Phillips, who was the only one of these
persons then in town. The *author* was so much
interested and encouraged by the conversation and
advice of the *bookseller*, that, without further hesitation, he offered him the publication of his work.
This apparently accidental introduction was a happy
circumstance for promoting the great cause of the
abolition, which its young champion had so much
at heart. For it led him to the knowledge of many
of those persons who afterwards became active partizans and useful auxiliaries in the holy warfare.
It was also important to him, immediately, as to
his work; as Mr. Phillips possessed acute penetra-
tion, solid judgment, and sound literary knowledge.
These qualities of the judicious bookseller were soon

proved by the excellent suggestions, alterations and improvements that he recommended in the additions to the original essay; which suggestions the learned author uniformly and thankfully adopted, after due consideration, from a conviction of their great value. It was advantageous to him also in another way, for it led to a lasting friendship between the author and his publisher, which remained uninterrupted till terminated by death.

Shortly after this introductory visit to the bookseller's shop in George Yard, Mr. Clarkson received an invitation to meet Mr. Dillwyn. At this first interview with his new friend, he met two or three other select members of this religious Society, who all appeared desirous to know the motives which actuated him in contending for the University prize. He frankly told them that he had, originally, no other motive than that which actuated other young men, so situated, and on such occasions; that was, the desire of being distinguished by his University, and of obtaining literary fame. But that he had,

since beginning the work, felt so deeply and acutely
on the subject, that he had taken it up as a matter
of imperative duty. This answer appeared to be
highly approved by all present, and much conversation ensued as to the best modes of forwarding the
great end, about which they had assembled.

As Mr. Dillwyn much wished to see his young
friend at his house in Walthamstow, he appointed
the 13th of March to spend the day with him there.
The conversation, for the most part, was on the subject of Clarkson's prize essay, and the consequences
that might ensue from it; and the author soon discovered the value of the treasure he had met with in
" friend Dillwyn," whose extensive knowledge, both
of the slave-trade and of slavery, as they existed
in the United States of America, which had just
obtained their own liberty, but which to this day,
in the seventieth year of their new-born freedom,
still hugs " the accursed thing" — slavery, to its
bosom, as if, instead of an imp of hell, it were a
babe of heaven.

G

From this well-informed man Clarkson obtained many important facts, which, by his permission, he introduced into his work. But how surprised and delighted was he, as he candidly admits, to hear, in the course of their conversation, of the previous labours, already noticed, of Mr. Granville Sharp, of the writings of Mr. Ramsay,* and of the controversy in which the latter had been engaged; of all which, he confesses, till that time he knew nothing. How surprised was he also, he says, to hear that William Dillwyn himself, with whom he was then conversing, had associated himself, two years before

---

* James Ramsay was a native of Aberdeenshire, born in 1733, and bred a surgeon, in which capacity he served on board a king's ship, but being disabled by an accident, he entered the Church and obtained a benefice in the island of St. Kitts. He resigned this preferment, and returned to England, when he obtained the rectory of Teston near Maidstone. Besides a volume of sermons adapted for the use of the navy, he published a treatise *On Signals ; On the duties of a Naval Officer ; On the Treatment, civil and religious, of the Negro Slaves*, 1784. He died in 1789.

that time, with five other friends, for the purpose of
enlightening the public mind upon this very subject.
How astonished was he, he exclaims, to find that a
society had been established in America for the same
laudable object; with some of whose leading members he was intimately acquainted. And he was
still more astonished at the inference which instantly
rushed across his mind that he was capable of being
made the great medium of connection between them
all.

These thoughts almost overpowered him, his mind
became overwhelmed with the idea that he had been
providentially directed to the house of his friend,
that the finger of GOD was beginning to be discern-
able in these several acts; that the day-star of
African liberty was rising, and that in all human
probability, he might be permitted to become an
humble instrument in promoting the great work of
the abolition of the slave-trade.

During the course of attending to the printing of
his work, Mr. Phillips, his publisher, introduced

him to Mr. Granville Sharp, the memoirs of whose
valuable life and patriotic services in the cause of
civil and religious liberty, have been ably recorded
by my amiable friend, the late Prince Hoare, Esq.,
formerly secretary for foreign correspondence to the
Royal Academy of Arts. The meeting of these two
friends of this righteous cause, must have been peculiarly interesting to both. Mr. Sharp, mature in
age, full of honours and renown; from his various
publications, legal, political and religious, especially
for his exertions in the case of the negro Somersett,
ranked among the master minds of the day; Clarkson,
an aspiring student, whose eyes had been opened,
and whose soul had been fired by the details of
cruelty and oppression, from which he sought materials for the composition of an academical essay, the
subject of which he knew little and cared less, except for the limited circle of university fame : both
zealously engaged in the same cause, to which the
elder was a born friend, and the younger a newly
convinced friend, burning with all the zeal of a new

convert. No man, then living, was more able to appreciate the value of Clarkson and his Ciceronian thesis, and how to guide and direct his powers, than Granville Sharp; and few men of the day were better able to appreciate the scholastic learning, or more ready to worship the brilliant halo which surrounded the hallowed name of Granville Sharp than Thomas Clarkson. They were born for and were useful to each other, one was the planet, the other the faithful satellite, revolving round its leader, and revolving in the same orbit, around the eternal sun of *Truth.* Clarkson, with his wild unrestrained ideas, might be compared to a young and luxuriant vine, swelling and branching into irregular twigs and bold excrescences, spending itself in leaves and ringlets, and affording but few clusters for the wine press; whilst the judicious and knowing Granville, was as the vine-dresser to the Lord of the vineyard, to cut the wild plant, and make it bleed, to grow more temperate in its vain expense of useless leaves, to be trained into fair and juicy branches, and to make amends for its loss of blood by an abundant return of fruit.

With this distinguished, practically useful man, Mr. Clarkson had many interviews and much intercourse, and in whom, he subsequently discovered, a relationship on the father's side. Mr. Phillips introduced him also, by letter, to the before-mentioned Mr. Ramsay, who, after much correspondence on the subject, came to London and visited him. This zealous publisher of good tidings, also introduced him to his cousin Richard Phillips, Esq., of Lincoln's Inn, who was then on the point of joining the Society of Friends. In this gentleman he found much sympathy of feeling and an earnest desire of being a co-operator in the cause of abolition. When Clarkson was gloomy and disheartened, Richard Phillips consoled and encouraged him; when animated by hope, his friend stimulated him, and he found in him a zealous, active and indefatigable colleague.

In the year 1786, Clarkson's work was completed,

under the title of "*An Essay on the Slavery and Commerce of the Human Species; particularly the African.* Translated from a Latin Dissertation, which was honoured with the first prize in the University of Cambridge, for the year 1785; with additions." It was published in the month of June, 1786, about twelve months after he had spoken the original in the Cambridge Senate-house.

Instead of waiting, as he at first intended, to see how the public received his dissertation, Mr. Clarkson, after his conference with Mr. Dillwyn, which continued to press weightily upon his mind, felt convinced of its inutility, and of the paramount necessity of beginning to work. He determined, therefore, to proceed forthwith; for he found that other persons were up and doing, and labouring heartily in the field. The harvest was ripe, but the labourers were few, they were however ardent; and an additional hand, though young and of small experience was an acquisition. He had been thrown suddenly among them, as if into a new world of kindred spirits; he firmly believed, also, that a way was being opened for him, under Providence, in which he was bound to walk, and that he should want support in his progress. He considered that he had now nothing to do, but to join in the holy work, and to procure as many fellow labourers as he could.

Having long enjoyed the estimable friendship of Mr. Bennet Langton, the friend and companion of Samuel Johnson, Edmund Burke, Jonas Hanway, Sir Joshua Reynolds, and other distinguished literary, political and public spirited men of the day, and who possessed the esteem and confidence of the King, Mr. Clarkson presented to his influential friend a copy of his book; anticipating therefrom, much good from its introduction into the hands of a man of such high character, and extensive connections in the higher circles of English society. The result answered his expectations, for when he waited upon his honoured friend, after he had read the work, he found that it had made a deep impression on the well constituted mind of Bennet Langton. As a friend to humanity, this gentleman lamented, feelingly, over the sufferings and miseries of the afflicted Africans ; and, as a friend to religion and morality, he abominated the crimes and cruelties of their tyrant owners. He cautioned the young champion of abolition, against being too sanguine in his expectations, as so many thousands of rich and powerful men were interested in maintaining the system and the traffic. Justice however, which he said, weighed with him far more than all private and political interests, demanded a public enquiry, and he promised Mr. Clarkson, his assistance to the utmost of his power. From that time forward, Bennet Langton became an active coadjutor in the cause of abolition, and so continued to the end of his life.

The next person to whom Mr. Clarkson presented a copy of his book, was the Rev. Dr. Baker, a learned and pious clergyman of the Church of England, with whom he had long been in the habits of intimacy. At this time, Dr. Baker was the popular minister of Mayfair Chapel, the congregation of which, consisted chiefly of persons of distinguished rank and fortune, and with the greater part of whom he was personally acquainted. This circumstance was of importance in the promotion of his views, and he was accordingly anxious to learn the opinions of so good and influential a man upon the subject of his dissertation. After the lapse of a month from the time' of presenting his book, he called upon his reverend friend; who did not wait to be asked for his co-operation, but offered his services in any way that Mr. Clarkson might think most useful. The Doctor added, that he felt it to be his duty to become an instrument to expose to the world, and to abolish such a direful complication of crime and misery. Dr. Baker became from that day till his death an ardent and active colleague.

The next person in succession who received a presentation copy from the author, was the then Lord Scarsdale, whose family he had known for about two years. Both Lord and Lady Scarsdale read the work attentively, and informed the donor that they were both desirous of assisting him in his labours, and in promoting the liberation of the poor Africans from their atrocious task-masters. Lady Scarsdale, at the risk of offending many near and dear connections, who had possessions or interests in the West Indies, considered it to be her duty, notwithstanding these circumstances to do so; and Lord Scarsdale assured Mr. Clarkson that should the question ever come before the House of Lords, it should receive his constant and utmost support.

During the time that Mr. Clarkson was thus engaged in making friends to the cause, he paid a visit, by invitation, to Mr. Ramsay at his rectory-house, Teston; and communicated the progress he had made in the goodly work. On hearing the account of these proceedings, his reverend friend was almost overwhelmed with joy. He told his young assistant, that he had long been of opinion, that the deliverance of the Africans from the bondage of this inhuman trade, was within the determined views of Providence, and that by calling public attention to their unparalleled misery, they would be instruments, under GOD, of originating the good work. Mr. Ramsay then informed his guest how long he had the cause at heart, what steps he had taken in making the world acquainted with its horrors; and, that having communicated his feelings to Admiral Sir Charles Middleton, afterwards Lord Barham, and his lady, the latter had urged him to write a work in behalf of these sufferers. This work Mr. Ramsay had began, in compliance with Lady Barham's importunities, and in obedience to the dictates of his own conscience; but fearing the censure and abuse which he foresaw would be heaped upon him for so doing, treat the subject in whatever way he might, he had, at one time, laid it aside. He had, however, recently resumed his labours at the solicitation of Dr. Porteus, at that time Bishop of Chester, and afterwards of London, after which, it was published in 1784.*

---

* This work may have been another stimulus to the Vice-Chancellor's proposed in the spring of 1785. See (*) p. 9.

Mr. Clarkson was delighted with this account of his reverend host's labours and feelings, gathering, from its tenor, that he might receive the aid of Bishop Porteus and Sir Charles Middleton, two new and influential friends of their righteous cause; to whom he was introduced shortly afterwards. During his stay at Teston Hall, Sir Charles Middleton's seat, he indulged in many solitary walks, and meditated, with an undivided mind, upon the importance of the measure, in which he was engaged. One day when at dinner with the family, he was so much delighted with the turn which the conversation had taken upon the subject, that he enthusiastically exclaimed, in the very joy of his heart, that *he was ready to devote himself entirely to the cause.* This resolution procured great commendation from the company, and Sir Charles added, that being at that time Comptroller of the Royal Navy, if Mr. Clarkson required any information upon the subject of his investigation, or any particular information as to Africa, he would obtain it for him, such as extracts from the journals of the ships of war stationed or cruising in those seas, or from other documents to be procured from that source, and that Mr. Clarkson should have free access to his office, for that purpose. This offer was gratefully accepted, and it operated as an additional encouragement for him to proceed.

The next morning, when Mr. Clarkson awoke, one of his first thoughts was, that *he had given a pledge to the Company*, on the preceding day. He, therefore, determined that *he would devote himself to the cause of the oppressed Africans.* He became uneasy at the reflection : he questioned himself, whether he had considered all things sufficiently, to enable him to go so far with propriety? He accordingly resolved to give the entire subject a full investigation, that he might not withdraw his hand from the plough, when he had undertaken to guide it. He therefore strayed to his usual solitary ambulatory in the groves of Teston, and meditated long and earnestly upon the exclusive subject of his thoughts.

Having reached a spot suited to his contempla-
tions, he began to calculate the contingencies that
might arise, and to balance both sides of the question; taking into consideration, among other things,
that he had not, as yet, obtained sufficient evidence
of facts, from which he might draw his conclusions,
and be enabled to undertake so great a task. But
he reflected, on the other hand, that Sir Charles
Middleton, had just then opened a new source of
information to him, that he would be assisted
by the local knowledge of Messrs. Ramsay and
Dillwyn, and that by his continued exertions more
would be acquired.

He considered, also, that he had not yet obtained
a sufficient number of active friends to support him
in his undertaking. This reflection caused him to
pass them in review before his mental vision. *First*,
he calculated upon the zeal and influence of Sir
Charles Middleton, who had a seat in the House of
Commons, and held the important office of Comptroller of the Royal Navy; next he felt assured of

the assistance of Bishop Porteus, who was a member of the House of Peers, as was Lord Scarsdale, who had also promised him his support. He had secured the important aid of Mr. Bennet Langton, who had an extensive and intimate acquaintance, with the leading members of both Houses of Parliament; add also that of Dr. Baker who had similar connections, and was possessed of great pastoral influence over his aristocratic flock. He could also depend on the valuable services of Mr. Granville Sharp, who stood so deservedly high in public estimation; James Phillips, his publisher, Richard Phillips the Barrister, William Dillwyn, the West India merchant, the Rev. James Ramsay, the Rector of Teston, and author of the before-mentioned work on the condition and sufferings of the African slaves in the West Indies; and also upon the compact band of brothers who formed the committee for abolition, and all the members of the society of friends. He thought, therefore, when he reviewed this goodly company, that bearing in mind the short time that he had been engaged in the work, he was well supported. He believed, also, that there were among his acquaintance, many whom he could persuade to interest themselves for the slaves against their oppressors; and he doubted not, that if he exerted himself diligently, many persons to whom he was a stranger might be raised up to act as able and zealous auxiliaries.

His next reflection was, that it was quite impossible that a great cause, like that into which he had voluntarily entered, could be promoted without large pecuniary means. He questioned whether a smaller sum than many thousands of pounds, would be sufficient to begin their operations; and asked himself whence such a sum could be procured? In answer to this important question, he persuaded himself that a sufficient number of generous persons might be found in this charitable and Christian country, who would unite with him and his friends, in contributing their aid towards the enterprize; and he felt confident, that as the benevolent Society

H

of Friends, had taken up the cause, as a religious question by a religious body, he might calculate upon their assistance in the righteous undertaking.

In the *last* place, he considered that if he embarked in the enterprize, he must devote himself wholely and solely to its duties. He felt assured that a little labour now and then, now a little and then a little, or alternate fits of zeal and apathy, would be inadequate to the end; and that where the worldly interests of so many thousands of persons would be affected by their interference in the unholy traffic, nothing but constant, unremitting activity would be demanded from him. He felt certain, that if the matter were taken up, there would be no hopes of its successful termination, unless it were by *one* who would make it the business of his life. He thought, also, that the span of one man's life, however it might be extended to its greatest length, might still be inadequate to its accomplishment. But he knew not any man who would devote himself and his entire time to the business. Sir Charles

Middleton, although so zealous and earnest in the cause, was largely occupied, in the execution of his official duties; Mr. Bennet Langton, occupied a considerable portion of his time in the education of his children; Dr. Baker had important claims upon him as a pastor, in the execution of his parochial and ecclesiastical duties; and his friends of the society, called Quakers, were most of them engaged in trade. He could *look*, therefore, *to no individual person from whom he could ask such a boon, but to himself;* and the question was, *whether he was prepared to make so great a sacrifice?* In support of the *affirmative*, he argued to himself, that there had never been any great cause undertaken by any man, in any country, or in any age so great and so important to religion and humanity, as that upon which he was meditating: that there never had been one in which more cruelty was inflicted, or more misery endured, or which cried more loudly to heaven and earth for redress. That there never had been a cause in which more good was to be done, no afflic-

tion in which the duty of Christian charity could be
so extensively exercised; never one more worthy
of the devotion of a whole life; and that if a man
thought wisely upon it, in all its bearings, he ought
to rejoice in being called into existence, were it only
permitted him to become an instrument to promote
its success, in any department of its machinery.

On the *contrary*, he urged to himself, that he had
been educated and designed for ordination in the
church, that he had already taken Deacon's orders
therein, that his prospects of success, through his
family and connections were both promising and
brilliant; and that by appearing to neglect or re-
nounce his sacred calling, his family would be dissatisfied, and, perhaps, unhappy.

These conflicting thoughts weighed heavily upon
his mind, and made the contest painful. The
sacrifice of his hopeful prospects, and the fear of
offending his friends, he confessed staggered him the
most of all the objections that occurred to him.
These discouraging views, and other difficulties

which arose in arguing the *negative* side of the proposition, dissipated all his enthusiasm, he says, as instantaneously as a flash of lightning, which was here and is gone. But the sense of duty and the holiness of his cause, nevertheless crept closer to his heart, and troubled him sorely. He acknowledges that he had ambition, that he had a thirst for fame, and a desire for worldly interests and honours, which he could not extinguish all at once.

In this state of mental perturbation and painful self-examination, did Clarkson remain in the umbrageous solitudes of Teston. At length the conflict ended, and the would-be Prelate yielded; not because he saw any reasonable prospect of success in his new career, for all cool-headed and cold-hearted men would have pronounced against it as visionary and Quixotic; but in obedience, he states,— and who can disbelieve him? to a higher power than human aspiration. "And this I can say," he emphatically adds, at the conclusion of his narrative of this internal conflict, "that both at the moment of this resolution, and for some time afterwards, I had more sublime and happy feelings than at any former period of my life."

Having thus determined on his future proceedings, he informed his friend Ramsay, that he should depart from Teston in a few days, that he might begin his operations, according to the pledge he had given.

In the autumn of 1786, shortly after this residence at Teston Hall,* and departure of Mr. Clarkson from his friend Ramsay's hospitable manse, the Rev. Cornelius Ignatius Latrobe, the venerable and venerated Pastor of the Society of United Brethren, Moravians, or Hernhütters, as they are variously called, who had a congregation in Fetter Lane, London, bears witness to the extraordinary effects of this visit. In a letter† addressed to his daughter,

---

* Since called Barham Court.

† Printed in the *Life of William Wilberforce*. By his sons, p. 79. Wherever this *Life* is quoted in this fragment, it is that published in *The Christian's Family Library*, 8vo., London, 1843, by Messrs. Seeley, Burnside and Seeley.

dated at sea, on board the *Albion*, the 5th of December, 1815, this excellent man after informing his daughter of various things connected with the abolition, Mr. Ramsay's transactions in the West Indies, his writings against this horrid traffic, and the shock which the details gave to Mrs. Bouverie, Ramsay's patron, and her friend Lady Middleton, etc., relates an animated conversation which took place during his visit at Teston, in the autumn of 1786. " Sorry I am," he writes, " that I did not mark the day when I was witness to that remarkable conversation, which took place at breakfast, Mr. Ramsay, if I mistake not, being present. Lady Middleton, addressing her husband, who was member for Rochester, said: "Sir Charles, I think you ought to bring the subject before the House, and demand enquiry into the nature of a traffic so disgraceful to the British character." Sir Charles granted the propriety of such an enquiry ; but observed, that the cause would be in bad hands if it were committed to him, who had never yet made one speech in the house; but he added, that he should strenuously support any able member who would undertake it."

This led to an interchange of opinions, respecting the willingness and fitness of several members who were named, to brave the storm, and defend the cause of humanity; when some one mentioned Mr. Wilberforce, *who had lately come out,* and not only displayed very superior talents and great eloquence, but was a decided and powerful advocate of the cause of religion, truth and virtue, and a friend of the minister.* He was then at Hull, and Lady Middleton prevailed on Sir Charles, immediately to write to him, and propose the subject. He did so, and communicated the letter he had written to the family, as well as Mr. Wilberforce's answer, which he received a few days after, " both of which," says Mr. Latrobe, " I heard with these mine ears." Mr. Wilberforce wrote to the following effect, " That he felt the great importance of the subject, and thought

---

* William Pitt.

himself unequal to the task allotted to him, but yet would not positively decline it;" adding, "that on his return to town, he would pay a visit to the family at Teston, and consult with Sir Charles and Lady Middleton, etc., on the subject."

"After Mr. Wilberforce's return from Yorkshire," continues Mr. Latrobe, " he visited the family at Teston, as proposed; and as *he endeavoured to make himself master of the subject*, and to obtain information from every accessible quarter, Sir Charles sent him to me,* to learn what had been effected by our Missionaries among the slaves, in the different West India islands; and I furnished him with every species of intelligence in my power."

Thus was an additional and powerful friend and ally, who afterwards was at the head of every conflict till the victory was won, added to the glorious cause, in the person of the eloquent, pure-minded, zealous Christian gentleman, William Wilberforce.

---

* Mr. Latrobe had been a zealous and efficient Missionary, himself.

# CHAPTER II.

---

"My ear is pain'd,
My soul is sick with every day's report
Of wrong and outrage with which earth is fill'd.
We have no slaves at home—then why abroad?"—

COWPER.

---

MR. CLARKSON RETURNS TO LONDON—COMMENCES ACTIVE
OPERATIONS—RESOLVES UPON THE DISTRIBUTION OF
HIS PRIZE ESSAY—VISITS AFRICAN SHIPS IN THE
THAMES—CALLS UPON VARIOUS MEMBERS OF PARLIA-
MENT—HIS FIRST INTRODUCTION TO MR. WILBERFORCE
—A COMMITTEE FORMED IN THE CITY, FOR THE ABO-
LITION OF THE SLAVE-TRADE, AMONG THE MEMBERS
OF THE SOCIETY OF FRIENDS—MEETING AT MR. BENNET
LANGTON'S — THE COMMITTEE APPOINTED AND COM-
MENCES OPERATIONS.

ON Mr. Clarkson's return to London, he called on
Mr. Dillwyn, to communicate the resolution he had
made, and the pledge he had given at Teston, and

found this gentleman at his town residence in the Poultry. He brought with him a letter from Sir Charles Middleton to Mr. Samuel Hoare, a member of the Quakers' committee for the abolition of the slave-trade, among the members of their own society. He called on this gentleman, at his town-house in Lombard Street, in company with Mr. Dillwyn, saw him, delivered his credentials, and had some conversation with him on the subject of his visit. The three friends then proceeded to Mr. Phillips, the bookseller, in George Yard, to whom Mr. Clarkson was desirous of communicating his resolution and pledge. They found him at home, conversing with a friend of the same society, whose name was Joseph Gurney Bevan. He communicated to them the object of his visit and received praise and encouragement from all; and made an engagement to meet them again, at the same place in three days.

In the evening of the same day, he waited upon Mr. Granville Sharp and made the same communication. That gentleman received the news with unaffected pleasure, and heartily wished that Mr. Clarkson might be blessed with strength to proceed in his arduous undertaking. Clarkson then took up his residence at the Baptist's Head Coffee-house, in Chancery Lane, that he might be near to the chambers of his learned coadjutor, Richard Phillips, Lincoln's Inn; from whose advice and assistance he had formed considerable expectations.

From the moment of his arrival in London, Mr. Clarkson abandoned every other pursuit, and devoted himself, exclusively, to the great and philanthropic undertaking in which he had embarked his life, his hopes, his prospects and his fortunes, with an earnestness and single-heartedness almost unparalleled.

The first discussion at his friend's chambers, was, what plan he ought to pursue to give the greatest effect to his resolution and pledge. After having argued the subject, two or three times, with his friend, they coincided in opinion, that as members of the two Houses of Parliament could act more powerfully from their legislative position than most

others in furthering the cause; it would be advisable
to distribute the remaining copies of Mr. Clarkson's
book among them, that by its perusal, they might
learn the atrocious nature of the traffic it exposed.
Also, that it would be expedient for Mr. Clarkson to
wait, personally, upon several of these eminent persons; and that he should endeavour in the mean
time, to increase his own knowledge of important
facts in the trade, that he might be able to answer
any objections that might be raised concerning the
question; as well as to be fully qualified to act as
Manager or Director of the operations to be pursued.

At the appointed time, the two friends, Thomas
Clarkson and Richard Phillips proceeded to George
Yard, Lombard Street, where they met the same
party of friends as before. Mr. Clarkson communicated to them, the result of their discussions
in Lincoln's Inn, relative to his proceedings in the
three different ways agreed upon by them; which
received the unanimous approbation of the meeting.
Mr. Bevan asked whether Mr. Clarkson intended to

distribute his books at his own expense? On being answered that such was his intention, Mr. Bevan immediately appealed to the company, whether it ought to be permitted? He asked whether, when a young man was giving up his entire time from morning till night, they, who applauded his zeal, approved his measures, and appeared desirous of acting with him, should allow him to make such a sacrifice? And whether, they would not, at the least, secure him from a pecuniary loss by the transaction? He therefore proposed that the remainder of the edition should be purchased by subscription; and that the author's feelings might not be hurt, by any supposed stain upon his character for receiving a profit from his work by this mode of disposal, the subscribers should pay, only, the prime cost of its execution.

Mr. Clarkson expressed his obligations for this kind consideration of his finances, and particularly for the latter part of the proposal, which relieved him from the fear of being suspected of a desire of gain by the transaction, and alone induced him to accept it. Mr. Samuel Hoare was then charged with the management of the subscription; and the books were distributed accordingly, principally by the hands of Messrs. Richard Phillips, and Bennet Langton, Dr. Baker, Lord and Lady Scarsdale, Sir Charles and Lady Middleton, and other influential advocates of the cause. Sir Herbert Mackintosh went, personally, to many of his friends in the House of Commons, Lord Newhaven did the same among his connections, and both of them distributed the books in high and influential quarters, as did also Lord Balgonie.

Lord Hawke, who informed Mr. Clarkson that he had long felt compassion for the sufferings of our African slaves, desired to be permitted to assist in the distribution, among the members of the Upper House, and Dr. Porteus, who had then been translated from the see of Chester to that of London, became an additional, and most efficient coadjutor in the work.

After having thus consigned the delivery of his book into the proper hands, Mr. Clarkson began to enlarge his qualifications for action, by increasing his stock of knowledge, particularly of incontrovertible facts. As he had obtained, according to his own account, the principal part of his information on that head from books, he determined for the future to see what could be seen of its horrors, with his own eyes, to obtain his knowledge from living persons, and obtain all that could be learned upon the subject, practically and personally.

Clarkson then began his active career; and with reference to the *first* of the before-mentioned points, the river Thames presented itself to his mind. Ships were occasionally departing from the Port of London to the coast of Africa; " and why," he said "can I not go on board such vessels, and examine them myself?" With these views, he made diligent enquiry, and heard of one that had just arrived from Africa. She was a small vessel, called *The Lively*, Captain Williamson, which traded with Africa, in the natural productions of that country, such as ivory, bees-wax, Malaguetta pepper, palm oil and dye woods. He obtained specimens of some of these articles, and now became possessed of those things of which he had previously only read. On conversing with the mate about the country, its inhabitants, productions, etc., that officer showed some samples of cloth, manufactured by the natives from cotton of their own cultivation, and sold him, after some persuasion, a piece of each sort.

This event created new feelings in favour of the afflicted Africans, particularly when he reflected that persons of so much ingenuity, who were able to execute such beautiful manufactures, should be carried into slavery against their will, and reduced to the level of brutes. The reflections that arose in Mr. Clarkson's mind, from this visit to the African trader, were principally directed to the better use that might be made of the great continent of Africa, and its teeming inhabitants, by substituting a more humane, and, at the same time, a more profitable

I

trade than that of stealing and selling human beings
like cattle. These views tended greatly to animate
and sustain him, amidst the labours of his vocation.

The next vessel visited by Mr. Clarkson was
*The Fly*, Captain Colley. Now he found himself,
for the first time, on the deck of a slave-ship. The
sight of the decks below, and of the gratings above,
of the barricades across the lower decks, and the
explanations of the purposes to which they were applied, and the reflection that such unhallowed practices were followed by Englishmen, by men who
professed and called themselves Christians, filled him
with melancholy, horror and shame. He found, he
relates in his narrative, soon after this investigation,
a fire of indignation kindled within him; and had
scarcely patience even to converse with the people on
board. He had not sufficient coolness to inspect lei-
surely the places that were open to him. He withdrew quickly from this den of horrors, and hastened
to meditate upon what he had seen and heard. But
those things which horrified him in the slave-ship,

produced the same effect upon his mind as the more agreeable things he had seen in the mercantile trader, animating and invigorating him for the contest.

During the time that he was engaged in these expeditions on the river, he was equally assiduous in investigating other sources of information, and in obtaining accurate intelligence, wherever it could be procured. Being ever on the alert, ever watchful for incidents, he often fell in casually with individuals from whom he gleaned some information to add to his stock. Every little increased his store, and he never suffered a day to pass without some attempt to enlarge his knowledge and to collect materials for his work. *Nulla dies sine lineâ* was his motto, and his daily accumulations of ammunition wherewith to exterminate the murderous traffic increased accordingly.

His great object was to see and converse with every one who had been in Africa, especially those persons who had never been interested in the slave-trade, or who, at any rate, were not then interested in its gains. In this attempt he was successful, for he soon obtained interviews with General Rooke and Lieutenant Dalrymple, of the British army, with Captain Fiddes of the Royal Engineers, with the Rev. John Newton,* then rector of St. Mary

---

* This extraordinary man, the friend and neighbour of the poet Cowper, and author of some admired theological works, went to sea when young with his father, who was master of a merchant-ship. He afterwards became commander of a slave-ship, in which he made several voyages to and from the coast of Africa and the West Indies in that inhuman traffic. In this degrading service he contracted habits of dissipation and vice, which the brutalizing trade in which he was engaged increased and confirmed. At length he grew serious and fond of study, relinquished his maritime pursuits, and obtained the office of tide-surveyor at Liverpool, wherein he continued several years. During the latter part of this period he became a preacher, and made several unsucccessful attempts to gain an appointment as pastor to some dissenting congregation. In 1764 he was ordained clergyman of the Church of England, by the Bishop of Lincoln, and appointed Curate of Olney, in Buckinghamshire, which he held for fifteen years. In 1779 he was preferred to the Rectory of St. Mary Woolnoth, which he held to his death in December, 1807.

Woolnoth, Lombard Street, with Mr. Nisbett, a surgeon, then residing in the Minories, with Mr. Devaynes, a merchant, who was in Parliament, and with many other persons from whom he obtained much valuable information on the subject of his enquiries.

By these means many important facts were obtained; the subject began to be developed more and more each succeeding day, and additions made to his accumulating fund of authentic documentary evidence. He made it an invariable rule to note down in writing, every day, all the facts he had gained, and, when possible, immediately after each succeeding interview and conference. Nor was he inattentive to the other objects of his vocation. To attain these he waited upon several members of Parliament. His first was paid to the benevolent Sir Richard Hill, Bart., of Hawkestone, Salop, brother of the Rev. Rowland Hill, and uncle of the gallant General Lord Hill. The Baronet was at that time county member for Salop, and was a frequent speaker principally on religious and philanthropic subjects in the House. At the very opening of the subject, Sir Richard warmly espoused the cause, as did other members upon whom he called. Some of them, however, he writes, appeared to make this profession of friendship to the cause more from the emotions of a good heart, revolting at the bare mention of such a criminal traffic, than from any knowledge concerning its inhuman details. One member of the lower House, the Hon. Mr. Powys, afterwards Lord Lilford, with whom he had been acquainted in Northamptonshire, seemed to have doubts of the facts stated in Mr. Clarkson's book, entirely from a belief that human nature* was incapable of proceeding to such a degree of wickedness and crime. Mr. Clarkson requested his friend to name any fact which he so doubted. Mr. Powys selected the case,

---

* In a debate on the abolition of the slave-trade in the House of Lords, the 24th of June, 1806, Lord (Chancellor) Erskine said, "that from his own knowledge there were cruelties in that traffic which no human imagination could exaggerate."

therein mentioned, of one hundred and thirty-two slaves having been thrown alive into the sea to defraud the underwriters. Mr. Clarkson thereupon promised to satisfy his friend fully upon that point, and sent immediately to Mr. Granville Sharp, who lent him his account of the trial,* as reported at

---

* This barbarous transaction was disclosed upon the trial of an insurance case, *Gregson and others against Gilbert and others*, before Lord Chief-Justice Mansfield, and Justices Wills and Buller, in the Court of King's Bench, at Guildhall, in the month of March, 1783. Messrs. Davenport, Pigot and Heywood were counsel for the insurers, and Messrs. Solicitor-General Lee and Chambre for the owners. The circumstances were as follow:—The ship *Zong*, Luke Collingwood, master, sailed from the island of St. Thomas, on the coast of Africa, on the 6th of September, 1781, with one hundred and forty-two slaves and seventeen whites on board, for Jamaica. On the 27th of November following, she fell in with that island, but instead of proceeding to some port, the master either through ignorance or a sinister intention, ran the ship to leeward, alleging that he mistook Jamaica for Hispaniola. Sickness and mortality had by this time taken place. Previously to the act for regulating the transport of slaves, these evils scarcely ever failed to carry off vast numbers during the voyage; the avarice of the traders inducing them to crowd or rather to *pack* too many slaves into the holds of their ships. On board the

large, from the notes of the short-hand writer whom
he had employed on that occasion. Mr. Powys read
the account, and became accordingly convinced of
Mr. Clarkson's assertion; and he declared, that if it

---

*Zong*, between the time of her leaving the coast of Africa, the
6th of September, and the 29th of November, 1781, upwards
of *sixty* slaves and *seven* white people died, and a great many
of the remaining slaves, on the day last mentioned, were sick of
some severe disorder, and *not likely to live long*. The dead
and the dying slaves, the consequences of this sickness and mortality, it must be remembered, would have been a loss to the
owners, and a proportion also to the captain of the ship, who
was allowed a certain *per centage* on the proceeds, unless some
pretence or expedient had been found to throw the loss upon
the insurers. The pretence herein alleged was the want of
water, which was not discovered till three days after they had
made Jamaica. Yet on the 29th, before any one had been
placed on short allowance, the master of the ship called the
officers together, and told them that "if the slaves died a natural
death, it would be the loss of the owners of the ship; but *if
they were thrown alive into the sea*, it would be the loss of the
underwriters;" and to palliate this inhuman proposal, the
master, Collingwood, argued that it would not be so cruel *to
throw the poor sick wretches into the sea* as to suffer them to
die a lingering death on board ship. Kelsall, the mate, objected
at the first, but Collingwood prevailed on the rest of the officers
and crew to the measure. On the same evening, in the night,

were true, there was nothing so horrible related of the trade which might not be believed. This gentleman became forthwith and ever after an active and useful coadjutor.

---

and during the two following days, he caused to be picked out of the ship's cargo, one hundred and thirty-two slaves, all or most of whom were sick, and commanded the crew by turns *to throw them overboard*, which order was readily complied with. It appeared by the evidence of Mr. Stubbs, late Governor of Anamaboe, then a passenger, and of Kelsall, the chief mate, that on the 29th of November fifty-four persons were actually thrown overboard alive, and that, on the following day, forty-two more were also thrown overboard alive. On the 1st of December, and *before the stock of water was consumed*, there fell a plentiful rain, which continued a day or two, and enabled them to collect six casks of water, which was *full* allowance for eleven days, or for twenty-two days on *half* allowance, and the ship reached Jamaica on the 22nd of December. They were also for thirteen days off the west-end of Jamaica, within two or three leagues, so that a boat could easily have been sent on shore for water even had the rain not providentially fallen upon them. Thus was it clearly demonstrated, the iniquity of pretending a necessity to put innocent men to death through the mere apprehension of a want of water, which pretended necessity never took place. Notwithstanding this almost miraculous supply of water by rain from heaven, they nevertheless *cast twenty-six more human beings alive* into the sea. This last act of this sad

The first interview between this young and in-
trepid champion of humanity and one of his ablest
friends and colleagues, Mr. Wilberforce, is an interesting feature in the lives of these distinguished phi-

---

tragedy was performed, as appeared by the evidence, in the sight
of many of these unhappy slaves, who were upon deck at the
time; and, fearing a similar fate, or a worse, being fettered,
*ten* of them leaped into the sea in despair and were drowned.

These facts, be it remembered, came out not upon the trial
of Collingwood for murder, as the justice of the case demanded,
but in a civil suit, instituted by the owners for the purpose of
recovering from the underwriters for the value of the slaves
thus cruelly murdered. But the strangest part of this strange
narrative is—that the owners gained their cause, and the perpetrators of this horrible deed were not even questioned *crimi-
nally* about it! The slaves were treated in a British court of
law as goods and chattels. Lord Erskine, when Chancellor, in
a debate on abolition of the slave-trade in the House of Lords,
on the 24th of June, 1806, concluded one of his glowing eloquent orations. " My lords, I have myself* seen these unhappy
creatures put together *in heaps* in the hold of a ship, which,
with every possible attention, must still be intolerable; and I
have heard *proved*, in courts of justice, *facts still more dreadful*,

---

* His lordship was four years a midshipman in the Royal
Navy, and afterwards six years in the army, four of which he
was with his regiment in the West Indies.

lanthropists; and an important fact in the history of the abolition of the slave-trade, and its demoniacal mother Slavery. At their first meeting, Mr. Wilberforce declared frankly that the subject had often

---

if possible, than those I have seen. Cases have occurred in which those victims of misery have been made frantic, and have sought death by violence, rising up in rebellion, and endeavouring to break the chains by which they were fastened to one another; and then have ensued scenes, *the bare statement of which is a disgrace to a British court of justice;* not to those who administer justice according to the rules of law; but to those who have the power of preventing, and who ought to prevent, a repetition of the misery, by putting an end to the practice by which it is produced. I allude to a case well known to my noble and learned friend (Lord Ellenborough) upon a policy of insurance, in which it became necessary to defend the underwriter from the effect of his insurance; for he had undertaken by his policy only to indemnify the assured in the usual way against the perils of the sea. The negroes on board the ship, the cargo of which was thus insured, rose in a mass to destroy the captain and his crew in order to liberate themselves. Having advanced in pursuit of their object, it became necessary to repel them by force, as well to save their lives, or as many of them as could be saved, as the lives of the crew. Some of them yielded, and some of them were killed in the scuffle. But many of them jumped into the sea, and were drowned; thus preferring death to the misery they felt on board; whilst others

occupied his thoughts, and was near and dear to his heart. Having read Mr. Clarkson's dissertation, Mr. Wilberforce, who was then member for the great and influential county of York, sent for the author, and expressed a desire to become acquainted with some of the authorities upon which he had founded his conclusions; which Clarkson supplied to the entire satisfaction of his enquirer. Mr. Wilber-

---

hung to the ship, repenting of their rashness, bewailing with frightful noises their horrid fate. Thus the whole ship exhibited nothing but one hideous scene of wretchedness. Those who were subdued into obedience, and secured in chains, were seized with flux, which carried off many. These things," said his lordship, " were proved on the trial before a British jury, which had to consider whether this was a loss which fell within the policy of insurance, the negroes being regarded as if they had been only a cargo of dead matter. My lords, many instances might also be given of mortality on board ships in this traffic, where the voyage having been unusually protracted, *famine has visited the ship, and death has kept pretty even pace with the short allowance!* My lords, these are scenes much too shocking to be described; and I ask your lordships, is it possible that you should voluntarily assent to the continuance of so much misery which you have the power of preventing; or, that you should deem this traffic consistent with humanity or justice? No, my lords, it is impossible."

force put some other necessary questions, and demanded whether the facts could be supported by evidence. On learning the affirmative, he wrote down the names of the witnesses, and sent for them ; and on hearing Mr. Clarkson's intention of devoting himself entirely to the cause, he paid him some handsome but just compliments upon his resolution, desired to see him on all necessary occasions, and to be informed of his progress from time to time. He also expressed his readiness to give him all the assistance in his power in the prosecution of his great undertaking.

The conduct and management of the various objects of his labours, together with the correspondence, taking down evidence, and other necessary details of the subjects, proved very laborious to Mr. Clarkson, and occupied a large portion of his time, being rarely engaged for less than sixteen hours a day. When he returned from Teston for the purpose of commencing operations in London, he promised his reverend friend, Mr. Ramsay, to send him a weekly account of his progress. At the end of the first week, his missive contained little more than what occupied one sheet of paper. At the close of the second week, the contents filled three; at the termination of the third week, six sheets scarcely sufficed. When the fourth week demanded its report, it was so voluminous, that he was compelled to abandon this hebdomadal task.

The encouragement of Mr. Wilberforce, and the patronage and assistance of other influential friends to the cause, led Mr. Clarkson to hope that it would soon become the subject of a Parliamentary enquiry. Meetings for its promotion were now held regularly at Mr. Phillips's chambers; and it was resolved that Mr. Clarkson should never lose sight of Mr. Wilberforce, whose talents, zeal and influence were held in such estimation, that Mr. Clarkson was advised to relinquish his visits and attentions to other members of the legislature, rather than fail in doing honour, and in paying due attention to the honourable member for the West Riding, whose eloquence, tact, high moral and Christian character, and attention to public business had raised him to the distinction of being a leading member in the House of Commons.

Clarkson and Phillips, who met together every evening at the chambers of the latter, now resolved to inform their friends in the city, upon whom the former occasionally called, that they believed the time was approaching, when it would be desirable to unite their labours and combine their forces. For if the abolition of the slave-trade was to be made the subject of Parliamentary investigation, with a view to its entire annihilation,* no one individual, however powerful in body, and resolute in heart would be able to execute the labours necessary to its accomplishment. It would demand the concentrated powers of many heads and hands, actuated by one mind. Besides, they asked, who could be

---

* The object of the Religious Society of Friends was then confined to its abolition among the members of their own brotherhood.

more fitted for such a combined energy, than those persons who had so generously, honourably and effectively laboured in the incipient struggle? In event of such a public and searching enquiry, large funds would be required for conducting it effectively, and what persons, they asked, were more able to raise and manage the finances, than bankers, merchants and rich traders, such as their city friends?

A meeting was accordingly held at Mr. James Phillips's house in the city, whereat Mr. Clarkson stated, that from the first hour his hopes began to rise, his view had always been directed towards the gentlemen then present, to be his fellow-labourers. Mr. Dillwyn replied, that from the first moment of their becoming acquainted with his Cambridge prize-essay, they had also directed their attention towards its author; and that from the time of their first meeting him till that moment, they had been actuated by a strong desire of coalescing with him, in the same way, which he now proposed to them. But that, in their opinion, matters did not appear sufficiently mature, to be arranged finally at that interview. The proposition, considered generally and as a preliminary measure, was, however, approved, and an assurance given to the two proposers that an union should take place as soon as it was considered seasonable. They also resolved that a weekly meeting should be held at the same place, to which Mr. Clarkson should report progress of his proceedings, and from which the committee could form a judgment of the proper time to assume the title of a united body. Pleased and satisfied with this arrangement, Mr. Clarkson returned, with renewed ardour, to his daily occupations.

In pursuit of the enlargement of his stock of knowledge, he had, by this time, gained access to the records of the Custom-house in London, from which he collected much valuable information. Having reason to believe that the slave-trade was peculiarly fatal to those persons who were engaged in it, he wished to procure copies of the muster-rolls of the crews of ships engaged in that traffic, from the Custom-house at Liverpool, for a given time. James Phillips therefore wrote to his friend William Rathbone, who resided there, to procure such documents. When they arrived, Mr. Clarkson and his friend Richard Phillips found the examination and abstracting them for use to be a long and tedious operation. The two friends generally commenced these dreary occupations at nine in the evening, after both had been fully occupied in the vocations of the day, and continued till one in the morning, and not unfrequently till three. When fatigued with their labours, they would sometimes, in the midst of them, and as a relief to their fatigued minds, take a stroll around the precincts of Lincoln's Inn, when all its inmates were fast asleep; and discuss, in the stilly silence of the night, the subjects of their previous lucubrations, and of the best means to be adopted to insure success to their righteous cause. "These scenes," says Clarkson in his narrative, "of our early friendship and exertions, I shall never forget. I often think of them, both with astonishment and pleasure."

Having thus recruited themselves they returned to their work, and from those muster-rolls, collected a mass of the most important information, as to the mortality among the crews of ships engaged in the trade. They ascertained, beyond the power of contradiction, that *more than half of the seamen, who went out with the ships in the slave-trade, did not return with them, and that of these so many perished as to amount to one fifth of all employed.* This was another important fact obtained for the opponents of this abominable traffic. As to what became of the remainder, the muster-rolls gave no account. This deficiency, therefore, provided them with subjects for further investigation.

With regard to the West Indian part of the question, Richard Phillips furnished much important information. He placed in Clarkson's hands several authentic documents concerning estates in those islands; obtained, principally, from the proprietors. These returns proved, that in plantations wherein the slaves had been managed by mild and prudent conduct, they had increased and multiplied to such an extent, as to supersede the necessity of purchasing any on those estates, thus rendering unnecessary the trade in human souls, and pointing to a practical method of abolishing the slave-trade.

From these new views and by the aid of this accumulation of facts, Clarkson began to see, as it were, with new eyes, with an enlarged sphere of vision, and with an increased focus. He was enabled, by them, to make many practical discriminations, to reconcile many things, which had previously appeared contradictory; and to answer many objections, which had hitherto assumed a formidable shape, and had been so many stumbling-blocks in his way. But above all, he was gratified at the consolatory thought, of being able, in a short time, to prove all that he had stated. Not that he had ever doubted of its truth, but it had been, hitherto, beyond his reach; but "Providence," he observes, "in ordaining laws relating to the agency of man, had never made that to be wise which was immoral; and that the slave-trade would be found as impolitic as it was inhuman and unjust.

In prosecuting his visits to members of Parliament, Mr. Clarkson was particularly attentive to Mr. Wilberforce and mindful of his suggestions. He found that liberal and enlightened statesman becoming daily more interested in the fate of Africa and of our West Indian colonies. He therefore presented to that distinguished advocate of humanity and of all that pertaineth thereunto, a full report of his progress and of the sentiments of those other members of Parliament whom he had consulted; of the feelings and dispositions of those earlier friends to the cause who were acting with them in the city; of the discoveries made from the returns of the London and Liverpool custom-houses; of the documents concerning the before-mentioned well cultured plantations in the West Indies and their favourable results; and indeed of all matters that had presented themselves to him and his able colleague, which he considered worthy of Mr. Wilberforce's attention, whose time was then much occupied in the important measures which were agitating the legislature and people of Great Britain.

Mr. Wilberforce had also been making enquiries for himself, which he freely communicated to Mr. Clarkson. This open and friendly intercourse between these kindred minds now became frequent, not a week passing without such an interview. At one of these conferences Mr. Clarkson suggested the propriety of holding occasional meetings of a few Parliamentary friends, to which Mr. Wilberforce assented, and such a particular meeting accordingly took place. At the first of these conferences, the following members of the Lower House and some early friends to the cause were present; namely, Mr. Wilberforce, the Hon. John Villiers,* Sir Charles

* Afterwards Earl of Clarendon.

Middleton, Sir Richard Hill, Mr. Granville Sharp, the Rev. James Ramsay, Dr. George Gregory,* and Mr. Clarkson.

At this preliminary meeting, Mr. Clarkson read a paper reciting the leading facts that he had obtained in his researches, with observations on the impolicy as well as the iniquity of the slave-trade. Many questions were asked, and much discussion arose out of the subjects related in the dissertation. To the questions, prompt and satisfactory answers were given; objections were started and freely canvassed; and, in short, the measures proposed, were found to be so necessary, that certain evenings as well as mornings were fixed for further discussions on the subject.

---

* This gentleman was a clergyman of the Church of England, descended from a Scottish family, born at Ferns in the county of Wexford, of which his father was prebendary. He obtained a curacy at Liverpool in 1778, where he published several excellent essays against the slave-trade. In 1782 he became curate, and in 1785 morning preacher at St Giles', Cripplegate.

Mr. Clarkson lost no time in reporting this satisfactory progress to his city friends; who became convinced that the time had now arrived for the proposed union, and the extension of their original plan; and conceived that it might be prudently effected, so soon as Mr. Wilberforce should give his word to move the question in Parliament. But, as that gentleman had not, as yet, given the least hint of such intention, Mr. Clarkson was requested to sound him thereon and to report the answer.

He therefore waited upon Mr. Wilberforce, but was so overpowered by the fear that his mission would be unsuccessful, or, at least, might involve him in a long and arduous controversy; and, also, by an awful sense of its importance, and of the responsibility imposed upon him, as it related to the welfare of countless thousands then alive, and of millions then unborn, that he was, at first, perfectly

---

In 1804 he was preferred to the living of West Ham in Essex, where he published his *Cyclopædia* and other works, and died in March 1808.

unable to mention the subject of his visit. He actually returned from his mission, without mentioning the errand on which he was sent.

In this melancholy state of mind, he called on Bennet Langton, and consulted him on the subject; who consented to invite Mr. Wilberforce and a few other influential men, to meet him at dinner; when, during the freedom of intercourse which such convivial parties admit, an opportunity might occur, or be created, to ask the question. The important day arrived, when Mr. Clarkson found himself at his friend's hospitable board, in company with Sir Charles Middleton, Mr. Wilberforce, Mr. Hawkins Browne, Mr. Windham, Sir Joshua Reynolds and Mr. Boswell. After dinner, the subject of the slave-trade was purposely introduced; many questions were put to Mr. Clarkson, who dilated upon each, in his answers, in order that he might inform and interest the company to the utmost in his power. The guests appeared to be greatly impressed with his account of the extraordinary loss of seamen in the trade, and especially with the samples of African cloth and other specimens of Negro manufacture, which he produced for their inspection.

Sir Joshua Reynolds, a great and distinguished example of the power of ingenious arts, in softening the human heart, gave his unqualified approbation to the proposition for abolishing the inhuman traffic; Mr. Hawkins Browne joined heartily in the sentiments of the great painter, and spoke with much feeling upon the horrors of the trade, which he pronounced to be barbarous, and contrary to every principle of policy, morality and religion. Mr. Boswell, after observing that the planters would urge that the Africans were made happier by being taken away from their native country to the West India islands, said, "Be it so! but we have no right to make people happy against their will." Mr. Windham, on hearing it suggested that the vast importance of our West India colonies and the greatness of our large commercial port of Liverpool would be brought to bear upon all who should propose or support the abolition of the slave-trade, replied, " We have nothing to do with the policy of the measure. Rather let Liverpool and the West India islands be swallowed up in the sea than this monstrous system of iniquity be carried on."*

During this interesting table talk, when every one appeared to be deeply interested in the cause, Mr. Langton put the awful question about which

---

* It is a remarkable feature in the history of human nature, that after such strong expressions, Mr. Boswell, in the following year, and Mr. Windham, after supporting abolition for three or four years, became inimical to the cause. The latter, however, returned to his former opinions; for in a debate on the abolition of the slave trade, in the House of Commons, on the 10th of June 1806, Mr. Windham, then Secretary of State, affirms, in his speech, that the slave-trade was contrary to justice, humanity and sound policy. That it was a great evil, that both the slave-trade and slavery, were each, *malum in se.* He did not think that the epithets, " Rapine, robbery and murder, at all misapplied to them. That although slavery was of such ancient usage, and had so long subsisted, he had no hesitation in declaring that it is a state not fit to subsist, because, *it gives to one human being, a greater power over another than is fit for any human being to possess.* Man is not fit to have so much power over his fellow creatures."

Clarkson had been so diffident, to Mr. Wilberforce, in the shape of a delicate and merited compliment; to which he replied that he had no objection to bring the measure forward in the House of Commons, when he was better prepared to support it, by arguments drawn from facts; provided, he said, that no more proper person could be found to propose it. Mr. Windham and Mr. Hawkins Browne both promised their support and interest.

Before leaving the company, Clarkson drew Mr. Wilberforce aside and solicited permission to announce this important determination to his friends in the city, of whom he had often spoken to him as being desirous of forming a committee, to consist of themselves and other warm friends of the abolition, to conduct the proceedings out of Parliament. The required permission* was given,

---

* Mr. Wilberforce records in his diary (see *Life*, by his sons, p. 83) : " When I had acquired so much information, I began to talk the matter over with Pitt and Grenville. Pitt recommended me to undertake its conduct as a subject suited to my

and Bennet Langton's dinner party separated with mutual satisfaction at its results.

On receiving this permission, Mr. Clarkson requested Mr. Langton to allow his name to be added to the committee, which having obtained, he departed highly delighted with his success. Having noted down, according to his custom, the occurrences of the day, he went on the following evening to the chambers of James Phillips, and requested him to call a meeting of their friends as soon as possible to receive his report. He also wrote to the Vice-Chancellor of Cambridge, Dr. Peckard, who had furnished him with the theme which called him to his beloved vocation, and waited upon Lord Scarsdale, Dr. Baker and other friends of the cause, to inform them of his success, and to enlist them into the society. He was successful in all these applications,

---

character and talents." The right reverend and venerable authors add, that "Mr. Wilberforce never divulged his determination, until at Mr. Bennet Langton's table, in answer to a question from his host, he avowed it publicly."

and was commissioned to act as the representative of these gentlemen at the meeting.

The meeting was accordingly held, Mr. Clarkson read the substance of the conversation at Bennet Langton's, from his minutes: no objections were made, no difficulty arose, and all present were unanimous for the formation of a committee of management. They met again, by agreement, on the following day for that purpose, and among other proceedings, passed a resolution that "The slave-trade was both impolitic and unjust." Also, " that the following persons be a committee for procuring such information and evidence, and for publishing the same, as may tend to the abolition of the slave-trade, and for directing the application of such monies as have been, and may hereafter be, collected for the above-named purposes."

Granville Sharp, *Chairman.*  William Dillwyn.
John Barton.  George Harrison.
Thomas Clarkson.  Samuel Hoare.

| | |
|---|---|
| Joseph Hooper. | Richard Phillips. |
| John Lloyd. | Philip Sansom. |
| James Phillips. | Joseph Woods.* |

All these gentlemen were present at this initiative meeting. Mr. Granville Sharp, whose name was placed at the head of the list, as the great patriarch of the cause in England, was, as such, solicited to take the chair. He is considered by Mr. Clarkson, in his personal narrative of these proceedings, as the sole representative of the *first* class of precursors and coadjutors in the work of abolition of the African slave-trade. Messrs. Dillwyn, Samuel Hoare, *Treasurer ;* Harrison, Lloyd and Woods, he considers as the committee, or representatives of the *second* class ; that is, of the people called Quakers of England. To this class he adds the name of Dr. Knowles, who was on the bed of death, but on hear-

---

* An eminent woollen draper in George Yard, Lombard Street, and father of Joseph Woods, jun., Architect, author of *Letters of an Architect*, and other esteemed works.

ing of the meeting, sent a message exhorting them to perseverance. The *third* class enumerated by him, is that of the Quakers of America, represented by William Dillwyn, who afterwards united them to the parent society in London, as corresponding members. Himself and Richard Phillips he considered as the representatives of the *fourth* class, most of which they had been the means of adding to to the society.

Thus, on the 22nd of May, 1787, the representatives of these four classes met together and associated themselves as the first acknowledged committee for the abolition of the African slave-trade. The committee, which, with Mr. Wilberforce as their chief in Parliament, with Pitt,* Grenville, Fox, Dolben,

---

* Concerning the services of this great Statesman, to the cause, Mr. Wilberforce, in a letter, written during illness to his friend, Christopher Wyvil, from Bath, says: "To you in strict confidence I will intrust, that Pitt, with a warmth of principle and friendship, that have made me love him better than I ever did before, has taken on himself the management of the business, and promises to do *all* for me, if I desire it, that, if I

Windham, etc., as his colleagues, accomplished, under Divine Providence, in a continued contest for twenty years, the great work of putting " an end to a trade which," as Clarkson says, " by measuring

---

were an efficient man, it would be proper for me to do my-self."—*Life of Wilberforce :* by his sons. And in a debate in the House of Commons on this question, on the 10th of June, 1806, five months after that great statesman's death, his political rival, Charles Fox, then Secretary of State, said in the course of his speech on opening the debate, and moving the abolition of the slave-trade, in allusion to his great predecessor, whose former services he recalled to his aid, that he could not refute some assertions made against his motion " more effectually than by referring to a splendid speech, which was delivered in this House by a right honourable gentleman (Mr. Pitt) now no longer among us. A speech which was the most powerful and convincing eloquence that ever adorned these walls ; a speech, not of vague and showy ornament, but of solid and irresistible argument, founded on a detail of indisputable facts, and unques-tionable calculations ; a speech, the very recital of which, would now conclude that subject, of which, however, it is impossible to give to those who had not the good fortune to be present on that memorable occasion anything but a faint idea ; a speech of which I would say with the Roman orator—

'Quid esset si ipsum audivisset !'

That, Sir, was a speech which was indeed remarkable, as were many others from the same person, for splendid eloquence, but

L

its magnitude by its crimes and sufferings, was the greatest practical evil that ever afflicted the human race."

All the members of this committee, were of the Society of Friends, familiarly called Quakers, except Granville Sharp, Philip Sansom and Thomas Clarkson. Joseph Gurney Bevan was present at the preceding meeting held the day before, when he expressed a desire to belong to the society, but wished to be excused from the arduous duties of a committee man.

After the formation of this committee the event was officially communicated to Mr. Wilberforce; and a friendship arose between them all, that remained uninterrupted, but as death thinned their numbers by calling them to rest after their labours.

---

as remarkable for solid sense and convincing reason, supported by calculations founded on facts and conclusions, drawn from premises, as correctly as if they had been mathematical propositions, all tending to prove that instead of the West India plantations suffering an injury, they would derive a material benefit by the abolition of the slave-trade."

# CHAPTER III.

---

"I would not have a *slave* to till my ground,
To carry me, to fan me while I sleep,
And tremble when I wake, for all the wealth
That sinews bought and sold have ever earn'd.
No! dear as freedom,—and in my heart's
Just estimation, prized above all price,—
I had much rather be, myself, the slave,
And wear the bonds, than fasten them on him."

COWPER.

---

PROCEEDINGS OF THE COMMITTEE—MR. CLARKSON PRO-
DUCES A SUMMARY VIEW OF THE SLAVE-TRADE, AND
OF THE PROBABLE CONSEQUENCES OF ITS ABOLITION
—A POEM UPON THE SUBJECT PRESENTED TO THE
SOCIETY BY ITS AUTHOR, W. ROSCOE, ESQ., OF LIVER-
POOL—IMPORTANT DISCUSSION AS TO THE ULTERIOR
OBJECTS OF THE COMMITTEE—IT DECIDES UPON ITS
PUBLIC TITLE—MR. CLARKSON DEPUTED TO VISIT BRIS-
TOL AND OTHER PLACES TO COLLECT FACTS—VISITS
BRISTOL, AND DISCOVERS THE ILL-USAGE OF SEAMEN
ENGAGED IN THE TRADE—OBTAINS OTHER IMPORTANT
INFORMATION — TREACHEROUS MURDER BY BRITISH

L 2

SLAVERS AT CALABAR—VISITS BRIDGEWATER ABOUT A
PETITION TO PARLIAMENT—RETURNS TO BRISTOL—
CONTINUATION OF THE SUBJECT TILL THE ABOLITION—
CONCLUSION—SKETCH OF THE ABOLITION OF SLAVERY
—DEATH OF MR. CLARKSON.

ON the 24th of May 1787, the committee again
assembled to proceed with the business for which it
was appointed; when, among other things, the
Treasurer, Samuel Hoare Esq, announced that the
subscriptions received, for the purposes of printing
and distributing the abridged essay, amounted to
one hundred and thirty-six pounds.   Mr. Clarkson,
having long before this meeting foreseen that his
enlarged dissertation on slavery and on the traffic in
human beings, was too copious for general circulation; and although a general diffusion of the horrid
facts which it contained was absolutely necessary for
the success of their abolition; determined, when a
committee was formed, to write a concise pamphlet
of some eight or ten pages to elucidate the subject.
He entitled it, *A Summary View of the Slave-trade,
and of the probable consequences of its abolition.*

He therefore presented and read his little work to this meeting; and after some discussion and a few additions, it was fully approved. Two thousand copies were ordered to be printed, with the names of the committee and a list of the subscribers, with the amount of their subscriptions; which were distributed in various parts of the kingdom.

On the 7th of June the committee met again for the dispatch of business; and, among other things, passed a vote of thanks to the Rev. Dr. Baker,* for his zealous and useful services in the cause. At this meeting, Mr. John Barton, a member of the committee, stated, that he was commissioned by the author of a poem, entitled, *The Wrongs of Africa,* to offer the profits of it to the committee. This agreeable offer, was thankfully accepted, particularly when they learned that it was from the pen of Mr. Roscoe, and its preface written by Dr. Currie,†

---

\* This gentleman had been, as before mentioned, one of Mr. Clarkson's earliest coadjutors.

† James Currie, M.D., F.R.S., etc., was born in Dum-

both inhabitants of Liverpool, the very nest and harbour of the slave-trade.

At this committee, ten of its twelve members were present; and an important discussion arose, as to a proper and permanent title for their society, so as to be expressive of its views. After a long and interesting debate, the committee were of opinion that they should define their object to be, The Abolition of the Slave-trade; not of slavery, which would naturally arise from it hereafter. Hence, from that day, and in allusion to the time of this decision, they resolved to style themselves, in all their adver-

---

frieshire, May 31, 1756. He resided for some time in Virginia, and became personally acquainted with the cruelties of the slave-trade. In 1781 he settled in Liverpool and obtained an extensive practice. His medical works were held in esteem by the members of his profession. In addition to this preface, he was author of a *Letter, Commercial and Political, addressed to the Right. Hon. William Pitt, by Jasper Wilson, Esq.*, which soon reached a second edition and obtained great celebrity. He is most favourably known by his admirable edition of the Works of Robert Burns, accompanied by a *Life of the great Scottish Bard*. Dr. Currie died of consumption at Sidmouth, in the 50th year of his age.

tisements, reports of proceedings, addresses, etc., although they were appointed in May,* "The Committee Instituted in June, 1787, for effecting the Abolition of the Slave-trade.

"Thus," says Mr. Clarkson in his narrative, "at the very outset, they took a ground which was for ever tenable; thus they were enabled to answer the objection, which was so constantly and so industriously circulated against them, that they were going to emancipate the slaves." This wise and prudent decision of the committee contributed greatly to the success of its cause; for Mr. Clarkson felt persuaded, that if they had adopted the other object, the extinction of slavery, they would not have been able, for a great number of years, if ever, to have accomplished their primary object.

---

* In the *Life of Wilberforce*, by his sonr, it is said, "Their first meeting was held on the 22nd May 1787, when Granville Sharpe was elected chairman of the twelve who met together, most of whom were London merchants, and all but three, Quakers."

Before the committee broke up, Mr. Clarkson represented the necessity of obtaining a greater knowledge of all those particular points, which belonged, naturally, to the object of their association; and among other measures, proposed that he should proceed forthwith to Bristol, Liverpool and Lancaster, there to reside for a time, to collect all the information he could obtain of the details of the traffic. This proposal was taken into consideration by the committee at their next meeting, on the 12th of June; when the propriety, nay the necessity, of his tour was apparent to every one; and Mr. Clarkson was unanimously requested to undertake it. The resolution was also ordered to be recorded in the minutes of their proceedings.

Having made due preparations for the journey, Mr. Clarkson took leave of each individual member of the committee. He waited, also, upon Mr. Wilberforce, who was then very ill and confined to his bed. Sir Richard Hill and some other intimate friends, were with him, in his chamber. After conversing as long as he could, in his weak state, he held out his hand to his enterprizing friend, bade him farewell, and wished him success. In *The Life of Wilberforce*, by his sons, alluding to this committee, it is said, " This body soon increased and became a valuable ally to Mr. Wilberforce.* It was long indeed before his name became enrolled amongst their number, because his exertions promised to be more effectual by his being independent of them." On leaving the sick bed of his valuable friend, Mr. Clarkson felt dejected and dispirited; as it appeared to him that it would be in this instance, as it often is in other mundane affairs, that we scarcely ever possess what we esteem a treasure but it is taken from us.

Mr. Clarkson determined to take this journey on horseback, not only from the relaxed state of his health arising from his long, close and constant ap-

---

* Rather, Mr. Wilberforce became a valuable ally to them; for they were first in the field.

plication to the duties of his task; but, also, because he desired to have all his time upon the road to himself, to meditate and to consider the best mode of forwarding the great cause.

Bristol was the first place of his mission, and on his way to that important city, when about a mile from its ancient towers, he became afflicted with feelings of the deepest melancholy, for which he could not account. He trembled, for the first time, at the magnitude of the task he had undertaken;* which was no less than to destroy one of the great branches of the wealth and prosperity of the important commercial city within whose walls he was about to be a resident. He began to reflect upon the numbers, power and prejudices of the people he should have to encounter; he anticipated persecution; he expected to meet " envy, hatred and malice

---

* Nor was Mr. Wilberforce less affected by similar feelings, for in a letter to his friend Wyvil, he wrote, " As to the slave-question, I do not like to touch on it, it is so big a one, it frightens me in my present weak state."—*Life*, by his sons.

and all uncharitableness" at every turn, and prayed
for a safe deliverance. He questioned, in his own
mind, whether he should ever leave the place alive.
But in journeying onwards, his mind became more
calm, his feelings more composed, and his spirits
rose from the depression into which they had sunk.
He considered, moreover, that these feelings were
profitable, inasmuch as they had convinced him of
the necessity of employing undaunted courage, activity and perseverance to insure success; and, above
all, to be watchful over his words and actions, and
to conduct himself so as to cause no stain upon the
holy cause in which he was engaged. When, therefore, he approached the city, he entered it with a
bold, undaunted spirit, and with a determination
that no toils should tire, no danger affright, nor
persecution deter him from his vocation.

Clarkson having now launched the vessel in which
he had been placed by her brave crew, as pilot, it
behoved him to become acquainted with the course
he had to steer, with the rocks and quicksands,

and all the perils that would assail him in this
voyage of discovery. His first introduction at
Liverpool was to Mr. Harry Gandy,* a newly admitted member of the Society of Friends. This
introduction was particularly serviceable, for Gandy
had been a sea-faring man, and in his youth of a
roving disposition. He had been two voyages, as
master of a slaver, of about 150 tons burden. In
the first voyage he took on board 120 slaves and in
the second 150, and went both voyages to the Island
of Santa Cruz; he lost a great many slaves in his
first voyage, and his crew were exceedingly sickly.
In a voyage which he made when a boy, there was
an insurrection among the negroes, who obtained

---

* This "convinced friend," in his evidence before the Lords
of the Committee of Council in 1788 and 1789, described himself "as one of the people calling themselves Quakers," lived
near thirty years in the West Indies, in the Danish Islands, and
made two voyages to the coast of Africa in the years 1758 and
1759; as Master of a vessel. Went to the river Gambia and
Sierra Leone, had been more than 200 miles up the river Gambia, but not more than 30 miles up the river Sierra Leone.
See *Report*, parts i. and ii.

possession of the ship; however, after many were killed, the rest were quelled, and many who were wounded were commanded to throw themselves overboard, which they did. They were fired upon by order of the Captain after they had surrendered. From this practical knowledge of the subject, Gandy was enabled to furnish Mr. Clarkson with many valuable particulars of the trade in Africa, and of the treatment and condition of the slaves in the West India plantations; and as he had frequently felt much compunction of conscience for the part he had taken in both, he felt himself, therefore, bound to forward the objects of the committee as much as was in his power, by way of reparation for his past offences, as he confessed, for the indiscreet and profane occupations of his youth.

Mr. Clarkson, received introductions also to the families of James Harford, John Lury, Matthew Wright, Philip Debels Tucket, Thomas Bonville and John Waring, all reputable members of the Society of Friends, and connected with the com-

mercial trade of Bristol. From all these friends he
derived much useful information, many important
facts and other assistance in his object. His enquiries were principally addressed towards ascertain-
ing what were the natural productions of Africa,
and to obtain, when possible, specimens of them,
and of native manufactures, for the purpose of forming a cabinet or collection of such articles. He also
sought information as to the mode of obtaining slaves
on the continent of Africa, of the manner of trans-
porting them to the West Indies, and of their treatment in the plantations. He was anxious, also, to
prevail upon persons who had knowledge of any of
these particulars to come forward as witnesses before
the Parliamentary Committee, should one be appointed.

To make himself still better informed as to the
loss of seamen employed in the slave-trade, he made
enquiries and took notes of the results in every
credible quarter. He also sought and obtained information as to the comparative loss of seamen em-

ployed in other branches of maritime commerce, from the port of Bristol, also the nature, quantity and value of the imports and exports of goods generally, and a few other facts, which he classed under the head miscellaneous.

In his first perambulations in and about Bristol, he found that the people spoke freely, and were very communicative about the slave-trade; that they appeared well acquainted with various circumstances relating to it; that there were certain facts concerning its horrors in everybody's mouth; that every one appeared to execrate it, but that no one thought of its abolition. He therefore pursued his object by examining the truth of these reports, and in tracing them to their sources.

On the 3rd of July, 1787, he was informed that the ship *Brothers*, then lying in the King's Road, bound for Africa, could not procure seamen for the voyage; and that a party of mariners which had been put on board, had been so terrified at the prospect of their employment from the preparations they

witnessed, that they left the ship in a body on a
Sunday morning. He was also told that of the crew
which had navigated that vessel in her previous
voyage, thirty-two had died, and that the whole had
been so barbarously used by the Captain, that he
could not now obtain hands. It was added, that the
general treatment of the sailors employed in the
slave-ships was a crying evil, and, consequently, few
would engage in it. So there was always great difficulty in procuring hands for this traffic, although
they were ready enough to enter ships engaged in
other trades.

These circumstances made Mr. Clarkson acquainted
with two striking facts with which he had previously
been unacquainted; namely, the aversion which
sailors had to engaging in slave-ships, and the ill
usage of them by their blood-thirsty officers, who
commanded these floating Pandemoniums. He therefore determined to investigate these facts thoroughly
and without delay.

Being unwilling, however, to lend too ready an

ear to bare reports, and having it in his power to ascertain the truth of one of them, the difficulty of procuring a crew for the good ship *Brothers*, he determined to do so. The cause of this difficulty, he apprehended, would furnish a key by which he might unlock the mystery in which this bloody traffic was shrouded, and provide a mark by which he might judge the degree of iniquity of its proceedings. He therefore obtained access, through his friend, Truman Harford, to the muster-roll of *The Brothers*. On looking over the names and descriptions of her former crew, he found the dreadful fact confirmed, that two and thirty of them were, during the voyage, numbered with the dead.

Having established that fact, he became exceedingly anxious to develop the hidden causes of the others, particularly the treatment of one of the crew, which, as reported to him, appeared beyond belief; and the consequent unwillingness of the sailors to engage on board a ship of such a diabolical character. The name of the man in question was John

M

Dean, a free negro. The account was, that for a trifling circumstance, in which he had taken no part, the captain had him laid, face downwards, upon the deck, and, whilst in that position, poured boiling pitch upon his naked back, and made incisions in his flesh with red-hot tongs. Before attempting to ascertain the truth of this barbarous proceeding, Mr. Clarkson determined to examine the ship's muster-roll again, to see if the name of such a man was there. He found it the last in the list, and that John Dean had been of the wretched crew, and had gone on board *The Brothers*, at Bristol, on the 22nd of July, 1785.

The next information obtained by this indefatigable man, was, that this very John Dean had but recently left Bristol for London. But he found out the landlord of the house wherein Dean had lodged, whose name was Donovan. On talking with this man upon the subject, he assured his interrogator, that the reported treatment of poor Dean by his captain was perfectly true; for, that during his residence with him he had a recital of his sufferings from some of his shipmates, and that he had often seen his seamed and mutilated back.

On asking Donovan if any other persons could corroborate this account, he referred Mr. Clarkson to a respectable tradesman who lived in the market-place. From this man he learned that he had long known John Dean, who was a sober, honest and industrious man, that he had seen the frightful scars and indentures in his back, and was told they were caused by the captain's atrocious cruelties in the way related, during the last voyage. This diabolical fact was further corroborated by Mr. Sydenham Teast, an eminent ship-builder, in the port of Bristol, who, not being aware of the extent of the captain's cruelty till it was developed on the trial, had become one of his bail in the action brought by the ill-treated African. Mr. Clarkson also obtained the name and address of the solicitor in London who conducted the cause for Dean, and was informed by that gentleman, at an interview on the subject, that it was true to the letter, and that he had made the captain of *The Brothers* pay heavy damages to his suffering client, as an insufficient compensation for the injuries he had sustained from that barbarian.

These abundant proofs of the truth of this transaction induced Mr. Clarkson to give more credit than he had done to the reports of the other barbarities practised in the slave-trade. It kindled a fire of indignation in his manly, feeling heart, and produced an ardent desire, a restless anxiety and a fixed determination to proceed in the undertaking. But what most excited these intense feelings of disgust and wrath was, that the purser (who, in Bristol, managed the out fitting of the ship, and directed what trade she should go into, and was often part-owner,) of *The Brothers*, knowing, as he did of these cruelties, should have sent this monster out again in command of her. This circumstance led him to conclude, that there must be a regular system of ill-usage towards the seamen engaged in this trade, that he could neither comprehend nor develop.

From Mr. Sydenham Teast, who aided him in this latter enquiry, he received much valuable information on the different natural productions and manufactured articles of the continent of Africa. This knowledge was obtained from the importations of his own vessels, which consisted principally of ivory, red-wood, cam-wood and gum-copal; but he purposed to import palm-oil, and knew that bees'-wax was to be collected abundantly on the coast. He gave Mr. Clarkson samples of the gum-copal, and some pieces of two sorts of unknown woods, which had the appearance of utility in the arts. One of Mr. Teast's captains had been informed by the natives, that cotton, of a pink colour in the pod, grew in their country, and he was of opinion that many valuable productions were to be found in the interior of the African continent.

Mr. Biggs, another ship-owner, in the port of

Bristol, who had one or two vessels, which skimmed, as it were, along the coast and entrances of rivers, in that quarter of the globe, for whatever goods or merchandize they could procure from the natives, without any connection with the slave-trade, also presented Mr. Clarkson with specimens* of Senegal gum, yellow-wood, malaquetta, cayenne pepper, samples of cloth, woven and dyed by the natives, the colouring matter of which was the production of

---

* It appeared from the evidence given before a select committee of the House of Commons, on the abolition of the slave-trade, in 1790 and 1791, that Africa had many noble productions to boast of: such as gum, wax, ivory, gold, cotton, indigo, tobacco, rice, pepper, sugar, woods, vegetables, and such like. Also, that the natives possessed a spirit of commerce, that they had industry and perseverance as traders, and that cultivation and civilization had uniformly proceeded in proportion to the encouragement given, and the demand for the articles produced. Here then we find both the *country* and the *natives* possessing all the requisites for commercial enterprize. The argument holds good now, in 1853, as it did in 1787, and shows the impolicy of the slave-trade, even as now, illicitly carried on, when so much and so many greater profits may arise from a legitimate trade with Africa.

the country. This gentleman felt confident from his own knowledge, and from the information of his people, that if competent persons were sent to Africa, with proper means, for the purpose of discovery, they would find it an inexhaustible mine of wealth in natural productions; and in none that would be more beneficial to us, as a manufacturing country, than in the numerous and beautiful dying materials that it could furnish.

From Thomas Bonville, he received two samples of cloth, made by the natives, and a beautiful piece of tulip-wood, a piece of another sort, which resembled mahogany, samples of fine rice, etc., all from Africa, presented to him by other friends to the cause.

Among other distinguished persons, whom Mr. Clarkson found in Bristol, friendly both to him and to the cause in which he was engaged, were Dr. Camplin, an eminent philanthropist of that city, who became his advocate and zealous defender against the calumnies and falsehood invented and promulgated against him by the African and West Indian slave-traders, as soon as they had discovered the nature of his mission to their blood-stained city; and the celebrated Dean Tucker,* who although then in his 76th year, felt great interest in the humane cause, expressed great sympathy for the poor suf-

---

* This great political writer was the son of a Welch gentleman, who cultivated his own estate, and was born therein in 1711. He was educated at St. John's College, Oxford, entered into holy orders, and was appointed to the curacy of the parish of All Saints, Bristol. Bishop Butler appointed him his chaplain, and obtained for him the Rectory of St. Stephen in the same city. His station in that seat of commerce caused him to turn his attention in that direction, and to publish many estimable works on the commerce of Great Britain, and that of other nations, the naturalization of foreign Protestants, etc. He proceeded to the degree of D.D. in 1755, and was made a prebend of the Cathedral Church of Bristol, to which was added the Deanery of Gloucester in 1758. In the disputes between Great Britain and her American colonies, he published several tracts thereon, in which he warmly condemned the opposition of the colonies to the authority of the mother country, but wisely recommended, at the beginning of the struggle, a separation between the two, and a formal recognition of the independence of the states by the British government. The Dean was also a zealous supporter of the abolition of the slave-trade. He died of paralysis in 1799, at the great age of 88 years.

ferers, and rendered much assistance through the veneration in which he was held by all. The Dean, having long moved in the political world, became desirous of knowing what of novelty was going forward therein, particularly as to the recent agitation against the horrors of the slave-trade, and the measures in progress for its abolition. Having passed a severe censure, in one of his tracts on the American war, upon the West India planters, for their inhuman conduct towards their slaves, he entered cordially into the views of the London committee for the abolition of the barbarous traffic. He, in furtherance of this object, introduced Mr. Clarkson to the leading authorities of the Bristol Custom House ; and made frequent calls upon him at the Merchants' Hall, whilst engaged in making selections and transcriptions from the muster-rolls of the seamen ; and, in short, interested himself in all his actions, and became an ardent and efficient advocate of him and of his cause.

The Rev. Henry Sulger, an amiable and learned

minister of the Gospel, in the religious society of
United Brethren, called Moravians, was also very
serviceable to Mr. Clarkson, in furnishing authentic
information of the cruelties practised by the slavers.
From this gentleman he received, for the first time,
unquestionable documents, and details of the treacherous massacre at Calabar, which had been frequently
mentioned to Mr. Clarkson, but with few particulars;
and as the transaction had taken place more than
twenty years before, he could not find a single person who had been present, or that knew anything of
it but by hearsay. This imperfect testimony was in
no way satisfactory to his inductive mind, for want
of authentic facts, as premises, whence to infer his
conclusions.

Mr. Sulger, however, removed this difficulty by
putting Mr. Clarkson in possession of authenticated
copies of the original depositions which had been
made and recorded in the case of *the King against
Lippincott and others*, relative to that horrible
carnage. These depositions were made by Captain

Floyd, of Bristol, who had been a witness of the scene, by Ephraim Robin John, and Ancona Robin Robin John, two African chiefs, who had been sufferers in the affray, and were taken before Jacob Kirby and Thomas Symons, esquires, Commissioners at Bristol, for taking affidavits in the Court of King's Bench.

The awful tragedy of which these three witnesses gave a circumstantial account was briefly as follows :—In the year 1767, six ships respectively named, *The Indian Queen*, *The Duke of York*, *The Nancy* and *The Concord*, of Bristol, *The Edgar*, of Liverpool, and *The Canterbury*, of London, were at anchor in the Old Calabar river. At that time there was a quarrel between the inhabitants of New Calabar and Old Calabar, respecting slaves. The captains of the vessels sent letters to the inhabitants of Old Town, particularly to Ephraim Robin John, the grandee or chief of the place, promising that if they would come on board, they, the captains, would become mediators between them and their enemies, the inhabitants of New Town. This offer was joyfully accepted, and the three brothers of the said grandee, first entered their canoe, attended by seven and twenty others, and followed by nine other canoes in the rear, directed their course to *The Indian Queen*, on board of which ship, the chiefs were received. The people in the other canoes were distributed on board of the other ships. The crew headed by their captain and his mates, armed with pistols and cutlasses, rushed into the cabin, with the intention of seizing the persons of their unsuspecting guests. These unhappy men, alarmed at this unexpected violation of the rights of hospitality, and struck with astonishment at the behaviour of their supposed friends, attempted to escape through the cabin windows; but, being wounded, they were captured and put in irons.

At the moment of this abominable treachery, the crew of *The Duke of York* fired into the canoe that was lying alongside of them, which instantly filled and sunk, and the miserable attendants upon the peaceful envoys were captured, killed or drowned. Most of the other ships followed this example, and great numbers of these wretched beings were slaughtered or taken prisoners. At this juncture, the inhabitants of New Town, who had concealed themselves, meanwhile, in the bushes by the river side, being in collusion with the faithless commanders of the ships, came from their coverts, and embarking in their canoes, made up to such of the miserable men as were swimming from the fire of the ships. The ships' boats were also manned and joined in the murderous hunt, butchering the greater part of those whom they caught. The result of this bloody carnage was, that, including those which were carried off as slaves, and those who were thus butchered in cold blood, all the principal inhabitants of Old Town were lost to their friends and relatives for ever.

This bloody act was scarcely concluded, when a canoe came off from New Town, full of its principal people, and demanded the person of Amboe Robin

John, brother of the grandee of Old Town, the elder of the three on board. The unfortunate man put the palms of his manacled hands together, and besought the commander of the ship, not further to violate the rights of hospitality, by surrendering an offending stranger, who had visited him in friendly confidence, to his bitterest enemies. But no intreaties could prevail with the stony-hearted slaver, who received from his sable allies of New Town, a slave named Econg in the stead of the chief's brother, who was forcibly carried into the canoe, when his head was immediately struck off in the sight of the crew and of his disconsolate and afflicted brothers, who escaped this fate only to be carried by their deceitful betrayers, as slaves and sold like cattle, with their attendants and companions, to the best bidder in the West Indies.

The confirmation of this tragical event, in all its treacherous and barbarous details, strengthened the belief which Mr. Clarkson had long entertained, that the hearts of those persons who were engaged in this soul-destroying traffic, became more hardened than in any other occupation in which mercy formed but a small ingredient; and that credence might, therefore, be given to narratives that had formerly appeared too atrocious for belief.* It made his blood boil with indignation against its perpetrators, and his heart sicken at the sufferings of the betrayed chieftains and people of Old Calabar. But he rejoiced, amidst the sorrows of his heart, that the time seemed to be approaching, when such atrocities would be first mitigated, and then finally abolished. This

---

* Among the circumstances given in evidence before a select committee of the House of Commons, in the years 1790 and 1791, it was proved that a slave-ship struck on the Morant keys at night. The officers and crew took to their boats, abandoned the vessel and reached land. The slaves on board got out of irons, made rafts and attempted to reach the shore, but were destroyed by the officers and crew as they attempted to make the land. Between three and four hundred were thus slaughtered, and only thirty-three or thirty-four of these kidnapped Africans were saved and taken to Kingston, witnesses of the wild and murderous tale! This case, among a thousand others, proves the heart-hardening effects of the slave-trade.

animating feeling gave fresh elasticity to his exertions, and he moreover rejoiced that he had visited Bristol.

In the course of his investigations in that city, he found reports current that the crew of the slave-ship *Alfred*, which had just returned from a voyage had been barbarously used; particularly a young man named Thomas, the surgeon's mate. It was stated that he had been repeatedly knocked down by the captain, and that in consequence of the ill-treatment which he had received, he had become so weary of his life, that he had three times jumped overboard to destroy himself, and put an end to his persecutions; that when rescued the last time, he had been chained to the ship's deck, where he remained night and day for a length of time. From this treatment his health had been so greatly impaired that he could not long survive the injuries he had received.

There was great difficulty in tracing this person, but Mr. Clarkson, with his wonted perseverance, discovered him, confined to his bed, and delirious. He could, therefore, collect nothing from this persecuted youth, relative to the particulars of his treatment; but in a few lucid intervals of brief duration, he exclaimed bitterly against the captain, and the chief mate. Pointing to his legs, thighs and other parts of his body, which were bandaged with cloths and flannel, he endeavoured to explain to his friendly visiter the extent of his sufferings. At times the poor sufferer said he forgave his barbarous persecutors, at other times he enquired whether Mr. Clarkson came to befriend him? And sometimes, with a wild distracted air asked if he intended to take the Captain's part, and to kill *him?*

Mr. Clarkson was greatly affected by the condition of this young man, his emaciated figure haunted him night and day; and whilst reflecting how he could most effectually assist him, he learned that the poor sufferer was removed from all his earthly pains by death. This circumstance stimulated him to look further into this affair, and in the course of his

N

inquiries, Walter Chandler, a member of the Society of Friends, who had been diligently searching for intelligence, found a young man, named Dixon, who had been one of the crew of the ship in question, and went with him to Mr. Clarkson. From Dixon, they learned all the particulars concerning the treatment of Thomas, the deceased surgeon's mate. The details differed very slightly from those which had been rumoured abroad. After investigating the seaman's evidence, so as to elicit the truth of the circumstances, he found no inconsistencies in the man's narration, nor prevarication in his manner of relating it. He asked Dixon, among other things, what caused the captain to treat his surgeon's mate, in particular, so barbarously. The reply was, that the captain used them all alike, except a man named Bulpin, who was the only one in the ship who had escaped ill-usage from the captain. In regard to himself, Dixon, he had been so cruelly treated in the early part of the outward passage, that he had, in a fit of desperation, thrown himself overboard.

When picked up, he was put in irons, and kept so confined for a long time. He was afterwards often ill-treated, even up to so late a date as within three or four days of their return to port. The captain had promised to make him some amends if he would be silent about the affair, but had not kept his promise.

Another seaman, who had belonged to the same vessel, named Matthew Pyke, related to Mr. Clarkson the whole particulars of the same cases, and also of the cruel treatment that he received during the voyage. His arm had been broken by the chief mate in Black River, Jamaica, and he had also been flogged, although contrary to the custom on board of merchant ships, by the captain's order. Mr. Clarkson considered it to be his duty to make strict inquiry into the characters of these men, before he produced them as witnesses of these facts. Of Dixon and Pyke, he could learn nothing, but he learned that Bulpin was a native of Bristol, and was of fair character.

This man was therefore sought, and found just as he was leaving Bristol for a distant part of the country. He was a young man of respectable appearance and mild demeanour, and as he was the only one of the crew who had not been ill-used, Mr. Clarkson expected that he could have no prejudice against the officers, nor inducement to falsify the truth of these reports. He confirmed the accuracy of the statements made in the cases of the surgeon's mate and the two seamen, and added that one, James Cunningham, had been a severe sufferer on board *The Alfred*, and that Charles Horseler, another of her crew, had been so severely beaten about the breast with the knotted end of a rope, that he died shortly after its infliction. He added, also, that it was a notorious fact that the captain of *The Alfred*, when he was mate of a slave-ship, had been tried at Barbadoes for the murder of one of his crew, but had escaped conviction by bribing the principal witness to keep out of the way. As a corroboration of this fact, and as an additional weight to Bulpin's testimony, Mr. Sampson who was surgeon's mate on board of the ship in which the captain of *The Alfred* was then serving as mate, confirmed it in every particular to Mr. Clarkson, and that he had often heard him boast in the cabin "how he had tricked the law on that occasion."

By these proceedings it may be perceived, that the further Mr. Clarkson advanced in the investigation of these foul deeds, the more diabolical did he find them ; and he saw no end to the dismal prospect which they opened to him. He thought at one time to have the captain apprehended and tried, either for the murder of the surgeon's mate, or of Horseler the seaman ; Pyke having the instrument of the latter's death, a rope with a knot as big as a large ball, in his possession.

Mr. Clarkson communicated these intentions to Mr. Burgess, an eminent attorney, and the deputy Town Clerk of Bristol, who had expressed an approbation of the cause ; but that gentleman proved the difficulty of the undertaking ; and added that he

knew but of one captain in the slave-trade, belonging to that port, who had not deserved hanging long
ago for similar crimes; but advised Mr. Clarkson to
delay his intentions for the present. This advice,
though judicious and prudent, Mr. Clarkson found
difficult to adopt, as his own disposition was such,
that whatever measures he engaged in he followed
up with burning zeal. He yielded, however, with
reluctance to the sound advice of his legal friend.
In his personal narrative, he places Mr. Burgess's
advice and his own fiery conclusions in juxtaposition,
with an evident predilection in favour of his own spirited resolutions; concluding with a remark that as
the passions which agitate the human heart, when
greatly inflamed, will find a vent, or will work off
as it were by subsiding or mixing again with the
original element, and thereby produce some new
passion or agitative fermentation; so that he found
the wrathful indignation, which had fretted his mind
against the murderer who had defrauded or evaded
the laws of man, subsiding into a temperate resolu-

tion of increased activity and perseverance for the future.

He began to think that the day was not long enough for him to work in. He often regretted the approach of night which suspended his labours, and joyfully welcomed the fresh and early morn that restored him to his occupations. When he felt weary, he refreshed himself with consolatory thoughts of the kindly nature of his work; and when disconsolate from the horrible recitals which poured down upon him, he found comfort in the cheering hopes of the result of the work of mercy on which he and his friends in London were then engaged. He lived in the animating hope that every day's toil brought him nearer to the haven of his expectations, and accordingly worked on regardless of trouble or danger.

Among other instances of the state of Africa, at the time of these incipient labours for the immediate mitigation and subsequent abolition of the African slave-trade, may be cited the evidence of Thomas

Poplett, Esq., an officer in the African corps, given before the Lords of the Committee of the Privy Council.* That gentleman was at Goree and Gambia, nearly four years, from 1779 the year of its reduction by the British forces to 1783 ; had been up the River Gambia to the distance of three hundred or four hundred miles, but never was up the River Senegal; had no concern in the trade himself, but had many opportunities of seeing how it was carried on. He stated the nature of the government of those countries, that is, the kingdoms of Demel, Tin, Barbessin and Barra, on the north side of the River Gambia, from the River Senegal to the Gambia, an extent of more than two hundred miles, to be all absolute monarchies, and governed more by the caprice of the monarch, than by any fixed system of government. They had, however, a council, which consisted of the alcaide or governor, the gerouff or

---

* Appointed on the 11th of February, 1788, to inquire concerning the state of the trade to Africa, and particularly the trade in slaves.

mayor, the marabou or priest, and some of the elders of the town, the entire council consisting of from seven to nine persons. These counsellors consult and advise the king, who was not obliged to follow their counsel, nor did he, unless it agreed with his own opinion, or interest, or he apprehended they had sufficient force to resist him, a power which Mr. Poplett said they frequently possessed and exercised.

To furnish the revenues of these kingdoms, every village paid a regular custom to the king, consisting of two descriptions of duties; the one annual and permanent, the amount of which was fixed by the king, and the other fluctuating, being in proportion to the trade of the ships. This revenue or custom was paid in slaves, with powder, shot, tobacco, brandy and other merchandize brought from Europe. When this custom was not paid regularly, the king, in the first place, gave notice to pay it forthwith, and if it were not paid within a certain time, he came down with force, and, as Mr. Poplett expresses it, "*breaks the village;*" that is, he took a great number of the inhabitants prisoners, whom he detains as pledges for payment. If the customary duties were paid he restored the prisoners, if not, he sold them for slaves. The kings, he said, never *broke* a village without some such pretence. They were understood to be absolute masters of the lives of their subjects; but they used that power with lenity; but when any of their subjects were represented by the alcaide, or chief of the village, as incorrigible, the king made no scruple of cutting off their heads without any form of trial.

The people of the coast he represented as being wholly Mahometans; next to these, in the interior, there was a country, the natives of which were called Sierrieurs, who believed in a Supreme Being, and testified such belief by showing great marks of joy and gratitude, on occasions of benefits received. They had no idols, nor any form of worship, their principal tenet was, that they are to be happy in this world, and they, consequently, endeavoured to make themselves so, by every species of licentious enjoyment, which they pursued even under affliction. The countries beyond this district were chiefly pagan. The country of the Sierrieurs was more populous, in proportion to its extent, than the Mahometan countries, and was governed by a number of independent chiefs, but had no king. The Sierrieurs were wanderers, like the Moors, but confined their excursions within the limits of their own country. The language of these countries, except that of the Sierrieurs was that called Wolloff, and was written in the Arabic character.

The black Mahometans of the coast, were described by Mr. Poplett, as strong and robust, very handsome and remarkably tall; woolly heads, aquiline noses and thin lips. The Barras were short and thick, with thick lips, flat noses and woolly heads; they spoke the Mundingo language. The Sierrieurs had noses quite flat, which they think a beauty, and press down the noses of their children to flatten them; were woolly headed, strongly built, short and thick. They tattooed their faces, were fond of war, and were a very artful people. The Wolloffs, he described, as a sensible, hospitable and civil people, but jealous and vindictive. The people of Tin, were serious in disposition, much oppressed by their king, and naturally jealous and vindictive. The Barbessins and Barras, he found to be an artful people, much accustomed to chicanery in trade, and perfidious in their dealings, lively, jealous and vindictive.

The men in general Mr. Poplett describes as very indolent; they did nothing but smoke, shoot and fish; the women did all the work of the field, as well as of the house. Every man was allowed to have as many wives as he pleased, if he could satisfy the marabou or priest that he was able to maintain them. The wives were, in general, slaves to the husbands, and worked very hard.

As one sample of the treatment of African slaves

in the West Indies, the following extracts from *Le Code\* Noir, dans les Colonies Françoises,* 1724, will be read with interest. De par le Roi. Ordonnances de Monseigneur le Duc de Penthievre, Amiral de France.

" Art. xiii.—Défendons aux èsclaves appartenans à différens maîtres de s'attrouper le jour, ou la nuit, etc., à peine de punition corporelle, qui ne pourra être moins que du fouet, et de la fleur-de-lys; et en cás de fréquentes récidives, et autre circonstances aggravantes pourront être *punis* de mort; ce que *nous laissons à l'arbitrage des juges.*†

---

\* Rightly named, for a blacker code can scarcely be imagined.

† " Art. xiii.—We forbid the slaves belonging to different masters from assembling together by day or night, on pain of corporal punishment, which will not be less than whipping and branding with the fleur-de-lys; and in case of frequent transgressions, with other aggravating circumstances, will be punished with death; which we leave to the decision of the judges.

" Art. xxvii.—The slave who shall strike either his master, or his mistress, the husband of his mistress, or their children,

" Art xxvii.—L'esclave qui aura* frappé son mâi-
tre, sa maitresse, le mari de sa maitresse, ou leurs
enfans, avec contusion ou effusion de sang ou au
visage, sera punit *de mort.*

---

causing a contusion, or effusion of blood, or on the face, will be
punished with death.

" Art. xxviii.—And as to any outrage or violence which may
be committed by the slaves against any person of the free population, they may cause them to be severely punished, and upon
such cases again occurring, even with death.

" Art. xxxii.—Any runaway slave who shall have been
absent a month, reckoning from the day that his master shall
have laid his information before the justice, shall have his ears
cut off, and be marked with a fleur-de-lys upon one shoulder ; and
if he repeats the same during another month, reckoning also
from the day of the declaration, he shall be hamstrung, and
marked with a fleur-de-lys on the other shoulder; and the third
time he will be punished with death.

* As a contrast, or rather parallel to this crime, let us look
at the then law of our own English colonies, where even the *murder* of a negro slave, when under *private* punishment, was *tolerated.* By the 329th Act of Barbadoes such punishment is
allowed, and by the same diabolical Act of Assembly, a man
who " may of *wantonness,* or of *bloody-mindedness, wilfully kill*
a negro or *other slave of his* own, he shall pay a fine of £15
sterling into the treasury."

" Art. xxviii.—Et quant aux exces et voies de fait qui seront comis par les esclaves contre les personnes libres, voulons qu'ils soient severement, meme de *mort,* s'il y échoit.

" Art. xxxii.—L'esclave fugitive qui aura été en fuite, pendant un mois ; à compter du jour que son maître l'aura denoncé à justice, aura *les oreilles coupées, et sera marqué d'une fleur-de-lys sur une epaule,* et s'ils récedive pendant un autre mois à compter pareillement du jòur de la denonciation, il aura *le jarret coupé,* et il sera marqué d'une fleur-de-lys sur l'autre epaule; et le troisieme fois il sera puni *de mort.*"

This *Code Noir* was first issued by " the most Christian king," " le Grand Monarque," by letters patent, dated March, 1696, wherein he states, " Louis, par le grace de Dieu (!) au milieu des soins que nous donnons à la défense de nos états contre toutes* les puissances de l'Europe, nous ne laissons

---

* France was then engaged against that formidable European

pas d'avoir l'attention nécessaire sur tout ce qui peut contribuer au biens denos peuples ; et particulierement sur le commerce, dont la continuation peut entretenir l'abondance dans le royaume, et y apporter les richesses étrangères ; et comme *celui* qui se fait au *Senegal* et sur *la cote d'Afrique*, et un *de plus considerables*, tant parle trafic de cuirs, gommes, cire, morphil, poudre, et matiêre d'or, et autre marchandises fines, que par les *negres*, qu'on porte aux isles de l'America, *si nécessaire pour le culture des sacres, tabac, coton, indigos*, et autres denrées qui sont apportées de ces pays en France, et dont *nos sujets tirent de si grands avantages.* Nous avons résolu de maintenir *ce commerce important,*" etc.*

---

coalition, under our King William III., which terminated in 1697, by the treaty of Ryswyck, by which Louis XIV. acknowledged his title to the English throne, and other important advantages to the powers of Europe.

　* " Louis, by the grace of God, in the midst of those cares which it causes us for the defence of our dominions against all the European powers, will defer no longer our necessary attention to matters which can contribute to the benefit of our subjects, and

The black or bloody code of the British government for its colonies was scarcely less atrocious, as
a few articles drawn from the legislative Acts of
Jamaica, Bardadoes, Antigua, etc., which received
the royal assent from British sovereigns will abundantly prove. By an Act of Virginia, (4 Anne, c.
xlix., § 37,) it was enacted, that "after proclamation
had been issued against slaves that ran away and
lie out, it was lawful for *any person* whatsoever to
*kill* and *destroy such slaves by such ways and means,*
*as he, she, or they shall think fit, without accusation,*

---

more particularly with regard to commerce, the continuance of
which will preserve abundance to us, and introduce foreign
goods into the kingdom; and like Senegal, which has become
one of the most considerable cities of Africa, as much through
trading in hides, gums, morphia, gold dust and other valuable
merchandize, as by the negroes that they import to the islands of
America, so necessary for the culture of sugar, tobacco, cotton,
indigo, and other commodities which are brought from those
countries into France, and from which our subjects receive so
many advantages. We have, therefore, resolved to maintain
this important traffic," etc.

*or impeachment of any crime for the same,"* etc. By another Act of the same state, (12 Geo. I., c. iv., § 8,) it was enacted, that if any poor fellow was taken up on suspicion of being a runaway slave, and committed to prison, the gaoler might let him out to hire, in order to pay the fees, even though he was not claimed, "and his master and owner remained unknown;" and in a succeeding clause, the gaoler is commanded to "*cause a strong iron collar to be put on the neck of such negro or runaway,* with the letters *P.G.* stamped thereon." In another clause, such unclaimed *runaways* were vested in the crown, and became king's negroes. By the 66th Act of Jamaica, the slave who ran away from his master or owner was "deemed rebellious," and a reward of £50 was offered to any one who should kill or bring in alive any rebellious slave.

By Acts of Parliament, colonial assemblies, etc., our British sovereigns were made to be slave-owners, and their slaves were called the king's

negroes; the 138th Act of Jamaica vested a number of negroes in the crown,* for the use of the
barracks, cutting and clearing roads, and other public works.   Twenty able negroes were allotted to
each of the twelve barracks in the island; were to be
paid for by a tax, and to be employed in building
barracks, etc.   The Receiver-General of the island
was to purchase negroes instead of those who died,
and gave other powers for that purpose.

Other Acts of Jamaica, enact laws for the management of their African slaves, among the bloody
provisions of which may be found in Act xxxvii.,
art. ii., that slaves *striking* a white person, were to
be punished with *death*.   Art. xiii.  "If arms, mis-
chievous weapons, or stolen goods were found in the
house or possession of a slave, he was to suffer *death*,
transportation, *dismemberment* or other punishment,
at the discretion of two justices and three free-
holders."   By Art. xx., if any transported slave

---

* Black diamonds of the crown, it may be presumed.

should return, he was to be taken up and executed. Art. xxii. " Commissioned officers to pursue *run-aways ;** to have forty shillings per head for slaves taken and brought in alive; and twenty shillings per head for slaves killed or driven home. Neglecting duty to forfeit £20." Art. xxx. enacted that, "if *any person shall kill a slave*, stealing or running away, that shall by night be found out of his owner's ground, road or path, and refuseth to submit: *such person shall not be liable to any damage or action for the same.*" Art. xl. of this Christian Act declared, that "no slave shall be free by becoming a Christian."

By the 64th Act of Jamaica, art. iv., if a slave had been one whole year in the island, and absented himself from his master for thirty days, he was " to be punished by *cutting off one of his feet.*" The

---

* Act xci., c. v., § 3, art. xvii., explained, that a slave who shall be found at the distance of eight miles from the house or plantation to which he belonged, without a ticket or other permit, was deemed a *runaway.*

66th Act of the same legislature, "for the encouragement of voluntary parties to suppress rebellious and
runaway negroes," empowered the governor of the
island to "commission persons to command parties
to pursue runaway slaves," had clauses of encouragement thereto, to hunters, etc. The 74th Act enacted
that if " any person clandestinely sending off this
island, or marking or defacing the mark of any other
person's slave, shall be punished by *death* without
benefit of clergy."

The manner in which their fellow-creatures ranked
with the Christian government of Jamaica (the other
West India islands agreeing therewith) may be seen
in the 103rd Act, art. x., which directed that *slaves
should be sold singly;* unless in cases of *families*,
when a man and his wife, his, her or their children,
were not to be sold singly; and *working cattle* to be
sold by the *yoke*, all others singly. Art. vi. of the
same Act re-enacted the "carrying off negroes" to be
" felony, without benefit of clergy." The preceding
Article, among " his Majesty's soldiers, white men

or women servants or *expressly* slaves." And by
the before-mentioned Act which "vested runaway
slaves, not claimed by their proprietors within a certain time, in his Majesty, to be employed in the service of the public," it was also enacted that the
Receiver-General should "collect all the *king's
negroes*,* and expose them *singly* to sale. The

---

* Among other proofs of the heart-hardening nature of the
slave-trade, the late General Sir John Doyle, introduced many
instances even among the softer sex, which occurred within his
own knowledge, when on military duty in Jamaica, and detailed
them, in a noble speech in the House of Commons, in the
debate on the slave-trade, on the 10th of February, 1807, he
said: "a neighbouring planter came into the camp, and I never
in all my life shall forget the tone and manner in which he made
his complaint, how spiteful his neighbours were." "Only
think," he said, "they have killed two of my negroes, and I
should not have thought so much about it, if they had not been
two of my very best negroes." "By the law of the island,"
said Sir John, "a person whose negro had been killed might
prosecute the offender, and recover a penalty, but this planter
told us that *he would not be so ungentlemanlike as to sue for
the fine*, but he would take an opportunity *to shoot a negro or
two*, belonging to the person, who had killed his, to balance the
account."

money to arise from such sale should be to his Majesty, for the support of the government." Thus making his Britannic Majesty, *de facto*, a slave-trader.

These instances, out of hundreds, noted for the proposed history of the slave-trade, and to be found in the *hundreds* of Acts of Jamaica and other British colonies, are enough for this fragment, or episode of the enormities put down by British philanthropy, and broadly show the causes which produced the desolating insurrections of St. Domingo and Jamaica. These were the legislators that called into existence the Dessalines, Christophes, Petions, l'Ouvertures, Rigauds, and other African and Mulatto slave-born or slave-made heroes of Hayti, the conquerors of Le Clerc, Rochambeau, and other French generals, and created the sable kings and able emperors of Hayti. These were the instigators of the Maroon insurgencies and devastating warfare between the English and the "*rebellious runaways*" of Jamaica, who, hated and despised as they were, compelled

British officers, bearing his Majesty's commission, to acknowledge these "black fellows" as captains, colonels, and chieftains, and to bring eternal infamy* on the West India Colonial governments of that day· "The vengeance of slaves," says Seneca, in a letter to one of his friends, " numbers not fewer victims than that of tyrants."

But a pleasing reverse may be found to this sad

---

* In the year 1717, when this disgraceful warfare began, the wild negroes or Maroons, as they were called, were in possession of three towns in the mountainous parts of Jamaica. The treaty with Cudjoe, was not made till 1738, nor completed with Quago till 1740. The legislature of Jamaica, were compelled to record its own discomfiture by their Act cxx., A.D. 1738, for confirming the treaty " executed by Colonel Guthrie and Sir Frederick Sadler, with Cudjoe the commander of the rebels," etc. Also, " Articles of pacification signed at the camp, near Trelawney Town, the 1st of March, 1738-9, including Captains Cudjoe Accompong, Johnny, Cuffee and Quaw, and"— *faugh*—" several other negroes." In 1740, they recorded in Act cxxvi., A.D 1740, " Articles of pacification between Colonel Bennett and Quao, the commander of the rebels," and other purposes connected therewith; and in 1741, Act cxxxiii., the Jamaican legislature, granted therein, " Further encouragement to Colouel Cudjoe and Captain Quaw."

monotony of barbarity in the following example of
an African imported into Jamaica, who refused to
return* to his home.

The late Sir Charles Price, having purchased
twenty newly imported negroes, had them brought
before him to be reviewed, soon after their arrival at
the plantation, whereon he intended to settle them.
As soon as they were all collected and arranged for
that purpose, he could not help being particularly
struck with the appearance of one man, whose looks
bespoke a mind labouring under severe affliction.
An irresistible curiosity prompted him to inquire
among the plantation slaves, for one of the same
country, who might perform the office of interpreter
between them.   A female linguist was soon found,
who put several questions to the disconsolate African,
dictated by her master, but to which he would not

---

* This narrative No. 4 of several papers transmitted by
Edward Long, Esq., to the before-mentioned committee of the
Privy Council.  See its *Report* of the 28th of March, 1789.
Part iii.

return any answer. The man turned a deaf ear to her expostulations, and seemed determined to maintain a sullen silence. In the meantime, Sir Charles, surveying the rest of his new purchase, remarked another man, whose air of cheerfulness promised better success. The proper inquiries were therefore addressed to him, and, from his replies, it was understood, that his disconsolate companion had been a cabocero, or chief of a village, in his own country, possessed of many slaves; "and I myself," continued the narrator, "was one of the number, and used to wait upon him every day." When this explanation was conveyed to Sir Charles, he was sensibly touched with the vicissitudes of fortune that had reduced this chief from a state of such elevation and authority in his own country, to be the companion in servitude with his own slave. Sir Charles immediately withdrew from the scene, sent for the carbocero to his house, and having received, by the means of a trustworthy interpreter, a confirmation of the story from the unfortunate chief's own mouth, he executed immediately a deed of manumission ; the purport of which was explained to him, accompanied by a declaration to the following effect :—" You are *now* no longer a slave, but at full liberty to go wherever you please. If it be your choice to return to your own country, I will endeavour to have you safely reconveyed ; but, if you prefer remaining *here*, your condition shall be as comfortable as I can render it." The astonished negro, in a transport of delight, fell on his knees, embraced the hands and feet of his benefactor, and bedewed them with tears of gratitude. Then thanking him in terms, the most expressive of his feelings, replied, " that as it was kindly left to his own option, whether to revisit Africa or to remain where he was, he would freely confess, that there was among his companions in slavery, a young negress, whom he wished to have for his wife, and if she would but consent, he would prefer staying in Jamaica, and ending his days with her."*

---

* How strongly does this incident prove the power and uni-

Sir Charles consulted the girl, she made no objection; a spot was assigned for their habitation upon a part of his estate, where they lived together very comfortably for many years. In the course of that period their happiness was increased by the birth of several children. Sir Charles's bounty did not end with his life; for in his will he bequeathed freedom to the wife and children, the father having been manumitted as before mentioned. Nor was that first act of liberality ill bestowed; for the grateful fellow conceived an inviolable attachment to the person and interest of his friend and patron, and was of great service in the rebellion of the negroes in 1760,

---

versality of the passion of love, the great instrument of nature ("God is love," 1 John iv. 8) the spirit of the universe, the master of the soul, be the body black or white, the object a negress or a Lydia. Horace aptly expresses it (lib i., carmen xiii. *Ad Lydiam*).

> "Felices ter et ampliùs
>     Quos irrupto tenet copula; nec malis
>     Divulsus querimonüs,
>         *Suprema citius solvet amor die.*"

when by the power of his influence over those who
belonged to Sir Charles's plantation, most of whom
were Coromantees, his countrymen, he effectually
restrained them from joining in the insurrection.
Well might the black Prince Dgiagola* write to his
" good white brother," that " black people are not
beasts, and do know how to be grateful."

But to return to Mr. Clarkson and his doings
in Bristol. Having been told, incidentally, that
the inhabitants of the town of Bridgewater in
Somersetshire, had in the preceding year, (1785)
sent a petition to parliament, praying for the abolition of the slave-trade, he determined, while his
feelings were so exasperated against it, by the horrors which he had developed, to go thither, and confer with the leading persons who had been concerned
in getting up the measure, considering them as true
and tried friends to the cause. He, therefore, proceeded on his mission with introductory letters to

---

* See p. 57.

Messrs. Ball, Sealey, Anstie, Chubb and other Abolitionists, in that place, and called upon them. He related to them, the atrocities which he had discovered, which filled them with feelings of indignation, similar to those which he had expressed; and they, thereupon, determined to present a second petition.

Mr. Clarkson, on his return to Bristol, resolved to investigate how far true the assertions were, that sailors had a dislike to engage in the slave-trade; and that they were sometimes inveigled by misrepresentations, and often forced against their will into the hateful employment. For this purpose he procured an introduction to a person named Thompson, who kept a public house called the *Seven Stars*. He was an intelligent, well informed man, who had been accustomed to receive sailors, as lodgers, when discharged from their ships, at the end of the voyage. He also provided them with board and other necessaries, till their vessels were again ready to receive them for a voyage; or, in the event of change, to

find berths for them on board of other ships. This
man avoided all connection with slave-traders, declaring that the credit of his house* would be ruined
if he were ever to send the seamen who entrusted
themselves and their affairs to him into that service.

From this person, Mr. Clarkson collected evidence
of facts sufficient to prove the truth of all that had
been related to him of this dislike on the part of
the seamen to enter into the slave-trade. But he
was not satisfied with hearsay evidence, and resolved
to make himself personally acquainted with the matter, and be his own evidence of the scenes enacted
on board the slave ships. He, therefore, accompanied by Landlord Thompson, commenced a tour of

---

* Sir John Doyle in the same speech noted in p. 198, seems
to have as degrading an opinion of the slave-trader, as mine
host of the *Seven Stars*, for after an elaborate and palpable
comparison of the apologists for the trade with an apology for
highwaymen, he said, " But, Sir, let me not be guilty of injustice, while pleading against it. I have myself been as uncourteously treated, by highwaymen as any gentleman in the
House, yet I should be sorry to *degrade their profession, by
drawing any comparison between them and slave-dealers.*"

inspection, and as there were at that time three or
four ships fitting out for the African slave-trade,
lying in the harbour, he found an excellent opportunity of satisfying his mind upon all his
doubts. These investigators generally commenced
their rounds about midnight, a fitting hour for their
dark mission; and employed themselves from that
time, till two, and, sometimes, three o'clock in the
morning. Thompson conducted Mr. Clarkson to
such of those public houses that were frequented
by the mates of the slave-ships, to pick up hands
and replenish their death-thinned crews. Those
petty pandemoniums were situated in Marsh Street
and were principally kept by Irishmen. The scenes
displayed in those horrid dens were abominable
enough in themselves, were sufficiently disgusting
even to Thompson, but to a mind constituted and
trained like Clarkson's were distressing and desolating. Notwithstanding ,these feelings, he was con-
scious that if he desired to learn practically and personally the transactions which he desired to hold up

to public execration, he could not retreat from his task, however revolting its labours might be. Music and dancing, the divine inspirer of the mind, and the most pleasing labour of the body, were here prostituted to the most infamous purposes; wine, given to cheer the heart of man, perverted by man's art to liquid fire, excited the fiercest, worst of human passions—drunkenness, lasciviousness and all debauchery; language, that great distinction of human nature, given to man as the aptest mode of intercommunicating thoughts, perverted to cursing, obscenity, blasphemy! Blessings turned into curses, tender mercies changed into bitter woes! Their "works lay hid in night;" night, the devil's day, was the high season of their orgies; and, in order to detect and expose them, it was necessary to be witness of their obscene rites.

The youthful mariner, if a stranger in the Port of Bristol, and uninformed 'of the nature of the slave-trade, was sure to be caught in the webs of these human spiders, who lay ensconced, seeking

P

whom they could seduce into their toils. Woe to the unhappy lad whom they caught; his doom was surely fixed, inevitable as death inexorable as hell. The beauty and accomplishments of their clipping craft hanging out its white sails, as emblems of purity, in heaven's fresh breezes, the exciting novelty of their undertaking, the pay! aye, the pay! the mammon of the mariner; the larger pay, offered so greatly above all others, the roving liberty on shore in collecting their *wares*, and other privileges and indulgencies, were among the baits displayed by these gulf hunters to catch aspirants for "barbaric pearl and gold."

Cheated in this manner, the unwary man was enticed into a boat that was always in due attendance, and carried off as a lawful prize; but if the flattering prospects that glared from afar before the intended victim, down whose devoted throat they poured the ruddy wine or more potent rum, for the black sacrifice, failed to produce the desired effects, if the blandishments of the demons and their damsels were insufficient to allure, good-fellowship as it was called, showing his plain face, bluntly spoke his mind, assumed the mask of rough sincerity, muddled his victim's senses with "the flowing bowl," whilst a bargain was being struck between the landlord and the mate for the price. Sometimes and not unseldom, "Solomon × Gull, his mark," duly or unduly attested, was produced to confirm the contract. When this step was gained, the new messmate was kept in drunken stupor that the landlord might be able to use his lodger as he pleased, and in due time he was handed over as one of the brave crew of the good ship *Tophet* of Bristol. Thus were slavers manned.

Seamen were also boarded in these public houses, who, when the slave-ships were going out, but at no other times, were encouraged, nay invited, to consume more of the commodities provided in such houses than they had money to pay for; and then were presented with the alternative offered, a prison or a slave-ship, the bilboes in Bristol or black-bird hunting in Africa. Sailors, generally, hate confinement and solitude, so the choice in this dilemma, was quickly made.

Mr. Clarkson and his competent guide were often witnesses of these atrocious deeds; for no fewer than nineteen such visitations,

"Fram'd and forc'd by need and accident,"

were made by them to those hateful haunts of vice and infamy; from which, from his own newly acquired experience, and from the information given him by Thompson and other persons well versed in the procuration of seamen, he found that no such practices existed, or were necessary for the manning of the mercantile navy, in any other traffic than the slave-trade.

General Gascoigne,* one of the members for

---

* Of this mercifully-minded legislator, Coleridge sung or said,
  "General Gascoigne's burning face
    He saw with consternation,
  And back to hell his way did he take,
  For the devil thought by a slight mistake,
    It was general conflagration."
                    *The Devil's Thoughts*, v. 17.

Liverpool, said, in the debate on the 10th of June, 1806, on a resolution for abolishing the slave-trade, among other bold assertions, "that as to the town of Liverpool, I say, it will be absolutely ruined by that abolition." Nearly half a century has elapsed since that fiery prediction, but how stands the town and trade of Liverpool in 1853? Its wealthy and liberal merchants and ship-owners, and its munificent corporation have given a satisfactory denial to the prophecy, by the extent and beauty of their public works. In the same debate Mr. Secretary Fox charged one of the gallant members for Liverpool,—for not less than two Generals* could suffice to fight for slavery,—with declaring in a former debate, "the slave-trade to be a thing good in itself; *so good, that if you had it not, you ought to create it by bounties!*" To this declaration the gallant combatant for slavery replied, in an after part of the same debate, "Now I come to the point

---

* The other was General Tarleton.

which the right honourable gentleman (Mr. Fox) reminded me of, which is a declaration of mine in this House, from which I do not shrink. What I said then, was what I shall now repeat, notwith-standing what has been said by that right honour-able gentleman, 'That, knowing the benefits that have resulted to this country from the slave-trade, I think it would have been advisable to institute rather than abolish such a trade;' for *I know*," added the General, emphatically, "*that if it had not been for that trade, this country never would have been in its present independent situation.*"

Let us look at the commercial, political, statistical and wealthy condition, internally and externally of the British Empire when under the prestiges of the General's much-be-praised trade, and its present state without it, or even its sable offspring slavery; now, thanks be to heaven and to its instruments, Granville Sharpe, Thomas Clarkson, and William Wilberforce, "themselves and fellows," happily and for ever abolished. The public official returns of the two periods have long and loudly proclaimed the difference.

In the course of the same debate, the other gallant member for Liverpool, General Tarleton, said among other things, that " the prosperity of Liverpool was intimately connected with the African slave-trade." As to the situation of Liverpool, he said, " It was once a mere fishing hamlet, but it has risen into prosperity in exact proportion to the extent of the African slave-trade, so as to become the second place in wealth and population in the British Empire. " Its exports," added the General authoritatively, "its exports, independent of the African slave-trade, were superior to any other port, except that of London, and the sum which it contributed to the public purse, was near three millions sterling, annually.

The correctness of this statement is not disputed; but if such was the magnitude of the commerce of Liverpool at that time, it is hard to believe that the abolition of the slave-trade could affect its prosperity in any material degree, as the subsequent results show, for the *entire* exports from Great Britain for the purpose of carrying on that traffic never amounted in the course of any one year to one million sterling. Our American friends would do well to examine these facts, and draw their deductions therefrom, if it were only on the question of profit and loss.

The General, in adverting to the necessity of compensation, argued that " there can be no pretence for refusing such compensation, because, whatever may be said about the injustice or inhumanity of that trade, it is not to be denied that *it is a trade which has been carried on under the auspices of this House and agreeably* to law;* and, therefore, if this trade is now abolished, all those who have carried it on must have their losses made up, particularly those who have been concerned in *building ships for the trade*, which, from *their peculiar construction*

---

* A palpable hit. See p. 193, etc.

*are unfit for any other :* and this compensation, I can assure his Majesty's ministers, *will be very considerable in its amount."**

If this were so, the ship-builders and owners were fraudulent breakers of the law, by eluding the humane provisions of the act for regulating that trade; slavers should not have differed from ordinary merchant-ships in any other respect than in having a somewhat greater height between decks, and therefore proves the converse of the General's proposition.

Another General Officer, the brave, humane and cheerful Sir John Doyle, took up this proposition in a subsequent debate on *The Bill for Abolishing the Slave-trade*, on the 10th of February,† 1807, when after putting the House in possession of his own

---

* This was shortly after the battle of Austerlitz, the assumption of the imperial purple by Napoleon, and his making three of his brothers kings; and the English treasury at a low ebb.

† It passed into a law on the 25th of March, 1807.

practical knowledge and experience of the consequences of this trade and of the condition of slavery
in the colonies, in addressing himself to that part of
the question, rejoined to both the gallant members
for Liverpool, General Gascoigne having reiterated
the proposition of General Tarleton. " Sir!" said
Sir John, " I am particularly glad that the honourable member for Liverpool happens to be in the
House to hear me, as I beg leave to observe that
what I am about to say forms a strong part of my
case. It was observed, Sir, by the counsel at the
bar and by my honourable friend (General Gascoigne) that Liverpool would be considerably injured
if the abolition were to take place. It was stated
that there were a number of ships built only for the
African trade, belonging to that port, which were
adapted solely to the purpose for which they were
built; and it was added, that there were also seamen, calculated solely for the navigation of those
slave-ships. We were also told that their harbours

and docks could be applied to nothing but the reception of slave-ships, never having been employed in any other way.

"Just let me see," said the gallant baronet, "for a moment, to what an extent that argument would carry us. I will suppose the case of a highwayman, who should have stopped some gentleman on the road, and robbed him; and being afterwards taken and called to account for his conduct he should have stated, 'It is true I did rob him and got the man's money, but you cannot blame me, for I know that if I had not committed the robbery, Bill Bagshot, who was further on the road, would. Sir, I am so accustomed to the trade, I understand so much about that sort of thing, that I should feel myself very awkward at any thing else. Besides I have gone to a great expense, I have laid out a great deal of money in it, and have bought four or five horses, which are good for nothing but to stop gentlemen on the road. I have not only done this but I have built stables for those horses, which can be applied to nothing but to hold highwaymen's horses; and my pistols are made only to stop gentlemen on the highway.' Such, Sir, might be the excuse of this depredator. But, Sir,* let me not be guilty of injustice while pleading against it. I have myself been as uncourteously treated by highwaymen as any gentleman in the House, yet I should be sorry to degrade their profession, between them and slave-dealers."

But there was a voice heard that night in the House of Commons, which though dead yet speaks, and adds more glory to Liverpool than a legion of slavery-supporting generals. The gentle but decided voice† of the Historian of Lorenzo the Magnificent

---

　* This point was quoted before, p. 198, (*) but it will bear repetition.

　† Mr. Roscoe could never thoroughly divest himself of his Lancastrian pronunciation, and when he was once discoursing eloquently in his country dialect, a member to whom he was a stranger asked Canning the name of the orator. " Hush," said the admiring statesman, " Lorenzo de Medici is speaking."

raised his voice in defence of his townsfolk and of humanity. "Sir," said Mr. Roscoe, "before I give my vote on this occasion, I am anxious to satisfy my own feelings, and in endeavouring to do so, I shall at the same time perform the duty I owe to the inhabitants of the town of Liverpool, which I have the honour to represent.

"Whatever may have been supposed of the interest or inclination of that corporation, they are by no means unanimous in support of the trade; but on the contrary, *a large\* and respectable body have voted for the abolition*, and I should disappoint their wishes if I were not to give my support to this bill."

After a statesmanlike survey of the question, which had occupied the public mind and the atten-

---

\* This assertion is corroborated in a letter from Dr. Currie of Liverpool, to Mr. Wilberforce, (see *Life*, by his sons, p. 153) wherein he writes, "You will, perhaps, be surprized that Liverpool does not petition for the trade. Liverpool will never again, I think, petition on this subject; *conviction of the truth has spread among us widely.* Tarleton is doing himself an injury he little suspects."

tion of the legislature a period of 20 years, he
argued against the barbarous and impolitic maxim,
that, "it is better to buy than to breed a slave,"
inveighing against those men, who promoted and
encouraged the dreadful wars by which the continent
of Africa had been so cruelly devastated to furnish
slaves for rapacious planters, as was well known to
every one; and that they had done so by supplying
them with the necessary implements of destruction,
and putting arms into their hands that they might
turn them against their fellow-creatures. "When,
Sir, this nefarious traffic is put an end to, when it
shall be no more their interest to deal in blood, there
will be some hope of peace and tranquillity being
restored, and the country itself improved." The
orator addressed himself to the vexed question of
compensation, which he considered should not be
confined to the narrow principle of compensation to
one side only; but they should remember, that
justice was due to the injured sons of Africa. He
further hoped and trusted that the time would come

when those parties who should be really injured by the operation of the bill would appear before that House, to receive such damages as they might be able to prove themselves entitled to.

Mr. Roscoe then concluded his effective speech which removed from the scutcheon of his native town some of those "gouts of blood," which the slave-trade had dropped upon its fair field, and which would have been perpetuated by their Gascoignes and Tarletons, could they have had their way, by observing, "I have spent my whole life in the town of Liverpool, and for thirty years* I have never ceased to oppose this nefarious traffic; and I consider it to be the greatest happiness and the most satisfactory event of my existence, that I am, on this important occasion, to join, not only with the friends of justice and humanity, but with the advocates of sound policy in putting an end to the African slave-trade."

---

* See p. 149, for the presentation by Mr. Roscoe to the London abolition committee of his Poem against the slave-trade.

The next object which demanded Mr. Clarkson's attention before he left Bristol was the treatment of the seamen on board ship, when employed in the slave-trade. He felt such interest in this matter that he resolved to make himself acquainted with their whole nautical history; for he had heard that they were not only personally ill-treated, but were robbed also of their nominally high wages, by being compelled to sign articles, that in case they should die, or be discharged during the voyage, the wages due to them at such time should be paid in the currency of the country whereto the vessel carried her cargo of slaves; and other like frauds; and moreover, they were not permitted to read the articles they had so signed.

To ascertain the truth of these allegations, Mr. Clarkson obtained possession of several of these iniquitous articles of agreement which had been signed and executed in former voyages of such ships, and other important documents which proved these fraudulent proceedings. Whatever branch of this system was examined, into whatever portion of this mystery of iniquity he turned his eyes, the more of barbarous cruelty did he find ; the whole trade being, in fact, a mass of deadly corruption from head to foot. He also employed himself in the Merchant's Hall in transcribing copies of the muster-rolls of ships sailing to different parts of the world, so that he might be enabled to make comparative estimates of the loss of seamen in the slave-trade, and of those engaged in other trades from the same port. By this effective process he found the importance of his enquiry ; for he was able, thereby, to prove that more seamen were lost by death on board of three slave-ships belonging to Bristol, in a given time, than in all other vessels, numerous as they were, that appertained to the same port.*

---

* The following abstract of such of the muster-rolls of Liverpool and Bristol slave-ships as were returned into the Custom Houses there, from September, 1784, to January 5th, 1790, will show the fearful mortality in that trade :—

Q

In visiting and inspecting various slave-ships, and becoming thereby acquainted with their constructions, fittings and dimensions, Mr. Clarkson was much struck, and deeply affected by those of two small sloops that were then fitting out for Africa. One was of twenty-five tons burden, and the other of *eleven* tons only, and was to carry *thirty* slaves!

| Periods. | No. of Ships. | OriginalCrews. | Died. | Returned of the original Crews. |
|---|---|---|---|---|
| From 1784—1785 | 74 | 2915 | 615 | 1279 |
| „ 1785—1786 | 62 | 2163 | 436 | 944 |
| „ 1786—1787 | 66 | 2136 | 433 | 1073 |
| „ 1787—1788 | 68 | 2422 | 623 | 1114 |
| „ 1788—1790, Jan. 5th | 80 | 2627 | 536 | 1350 |
| Total | 350 | 12263 | 2643 | 5760 |

By this account it appears that more than *one fifth* of the original crews died during the voyage, exclusive of those which were left in the West Indies, which amounted nearly to one half, being, as reported in the evidence, "sickly, emaciated, destitute and dying!"

and at the end of their venture to be sold as pleasure yachts, for which purpose indeed they were originally built.

Among his greatest difficulties was the uncertainty whether he could insure the attendance of those persons who had been personally acquainted with the mysterious iniquities of the traffic, if called upon to give evidence of their knowledge before the constituted authorities in London. Friend Harry Gandy* had been, as noticed before,† long resident in the West Indies, had been two voyages as master of a slave-ship to and from Africa, and although much advanced in age, declared his willingness to go to London, and publicly declare all that he knew of it, both in Africa and in the West Indies. With regard to many others from whom he had gained intelligence in Bristol, and some who had been on the coast of Africa, with whom he had become ac-

---

* This person did give useful evidence before the Privy Council Committee in 1788.  See its *Report*.

† Page 156.

Q 2

quainted in that place, with the exception of the converted Harry Gandy, he had not, at that time, met *one* who would come forward as a witness. All his endeavours to prevail on them to give evidence thereon was fruitless. He sent messages to them by various friends, he met their views and combatted their objections in all ways, he told them that if there was nothing objectionable in the trade, seeing that it lay under a disgraceful stigma, they would have by compliance a proper opportunity of removing it. If, on the contrary, it was as iniquitous and impolitic as reported, *then* they would have it in their power to correct a glaring evil by exposing the crimes that had hitherto damaged it, and cause some reparation or atonement to be made for its former evils.

But he found that no representations he could make, no arguments he could use, were of any effect. Intercourse was thenceforward forbidden, and whenever he met them in the streets they shunned him as if he had a contagious fever. To continue the details of Mr. Clarkson's labours, in the collection of materials for evidence to be laid before the government and the legislature of the country, would be to convert this monograph into that general history of the abolition of which it is only a contributory fragment. It is indeed a sad eventful history, overflowing at every turn with the most abominable atrocities, treacheries, rapine, blood and murder, that ever disgraced a civilized nation calling itself Christian. But Britain when informed of its heart-rending details, gloriously shook off the deadly incubus, and by giving freedom to the slave made all her subjects free, and relieved her honoured flag from the fetter and the whip.

Clarkson returned from his mission, and laid the voluminous results of his labours before the London committee of which he was so marked and distinguished a member. Their task so far accomplished, the society fell into the rear rank of the parliamentary forces, and prompted and otherways assisted their leaders as the warfare proceeded.

The public attention had been roused and stimulated to a consideration of the slave-trade by the numerous pamphlets and books, published by Mr. Granville Sharp, Mr. Clarkson and the committee to which they belonged, pointing out its injustice, inhumanity and impolicy, and recommending its abolition; and petitions to the same effect had been presented to Parliament. Mr. Wilberforce had, as before stated, stood forward as a volunteer in the service of the Africans; and the discussions which had arisen on the presentation of these numerous petitions* from the country adherents of the abolition, induced Mr. Pitt, at the request of Mr. Wilberforce, who was then seriously ill† at Bath, to

---

* In *The Life of Wilberforce*, by his Sons, p. 92, "The number of these petitions are stated to be no fewer than one hundred to the House of Commons."

† So ill, indeed, as to be unable to read any letters on business, and the epistle in his name, committing the conduct of the business to Mr. Pitt, was written by Mrs. Wilberforce, Miss Bird and Mr. Hawkins Brown. See *Life of Wilberforce*, by his Sons, p. 93.

recommend it to the notice of the king (George III.) who appointed on the 11th of February, 1788, by an order in council, a committee to consider forthwith the state of the African trade, particularly as to the practice and manner of purchasing or obtaining slaves on the coast of Africa, and the importation and sale of such slaves, either in the British colonies or settlements, or in the foreign colonies and settlements, in America or the West Indies; and for other important inquiries mentioned in that order in council.* This committee of the Privy Council proceeded immediately to examine the various facts and allegations contained in the representations, as well of the friends of the abolition of the trade as of those who defended its expediency and justice.

On the 9th of May following the appointment of this royal commission, Mr. Pitt moved the following

---

* The Lords of this Committee of Council, among which Bishop Porteus greatly distinguished himself, submitted their report to the king in council, on the 28th of March, 1789. It was printed by order immediately in one large volume folio.

resolution in the House of Commons :—"That this House will, early in the next session of Parliament, proceed to take into consideration the circumstances of the slave-trade complained of in the petitions presented to the House, and what may be fit to be done thereupon." Before that time arrived, Mr. Pitt informed the House, that the inquiry instituted before the Privy Council would be brought to such a state of maturity as to make it proper that the result of it should be communicated to the House, in order to facilitate their investigation, and to enable them to proceed to a decision founded equally upon principles of humanity, justice and sound policy.

The examination of the matter by the Privy Council was strongly reprobated by Mr. Burke and Mr. Fox, both of whom insisted that the examination of the matter of petitions presented to the House of Commons should rest solely with the House itself. In a conversation that ensued, Sir William Dolben called upon the House to alleviate, by some salutary legislative regulations, the sufferings of the negroes in their passage from Africa to the West Indies. The House having expressed their concurrence with that gentleman's sentiments on this subject, he afterwards brought in a bill to fix the number of slaves which each ship in the trade should contain, according to its tonnage, to secure to them an ample supply of provisions during their passage, and to provide other means for the better preservation of their comfort and health. This bill, with some useful amendments, was carried to the House of Lords on the 10th of June, was passed into a law, and became the first-fruits of Mr. Clarkson's mission to the slave-dealing out-ports of the kingdom.

Early in the parliamentary session of 1791, a committee had been appointed, on the motion of Mr. Wilberforce, for receiving and examining evidence on the subject of the slave-trade, as a preliminary measure to another motion for its abolition.* A

* Mr Wilberforce had made a motion to the same purport, on the 12th of May, 1789, after an eloquent and effective speech of three hours and a half duration, in which he went

great mass of evidence had been collected during the preceding and in the early part of the then session, principally by Mr. Wilberforce and Mr. William Smith, the member for Norwich, and on the 19th of April, Mr. Wilberforce moved for leave to bring in a bill for that purpose. Mr. Pitt spoke with his usual eloquence, and with evident earnestness in favour of the motion. He declared that in all the questions, whether political or personal, in which he had ever engaged, there never had been one, in which his heart had been so deeply interested as in that before the House; both on account of the serious principles which it involved, and of the

---

over the whole subject; and moved twelve resolutions, which were entered on the Journals of the House. On the 21st of May the discussion was resumed, and after a debate of unusual warmth, the West India interest succeeded in deferring the decision of the House, till counsel had been heard and evidence given at the bar. This measure lasted till the 22nd of June, when, owing to the lateness of the session, it was postponed till the following year. He records in his Diary of May 11th, "Went to Montagu's with Burgh, where also were Ramsay and Clarkson."—*Life*, by his Sons, p. 112.

important consequences with which it was connected. He argued the question on the twofold ground of justice and of policy. Convinced as he was that the trade was founded on injustice, it was impossible for him to give his support to its continuance, unless he could be convinced that there were no laws of morality binding upon nations, and that it was no duty of a legislature to restrain its subjects from invading the happiness of other countries, and from violating the fundamental principles of justice. The arguments and interest* of its opponents prevailed, and the motion for abolishing the trade was negatived by a majority of 163 to 88.

"With this adverse decision," say the filial authors of *The Life of Wilberforce*, "all attempts to carry the case further in the House of Commons ended for this session. It had now become necessary to appeal to the justice and humanity of the nation, for that redress which was denied by the

---

* See Burke's fear of that interest, p. 3.

policy of Parliament. Mr. Clarkson and Dr. Dickson were accordingly dispatched upon provincial tours, for the purpose of disseminating widely an *Abstract of the Evidence given before the House of Commons' Committee*, and *The Substance of the Debate in the House of Commons, on the* 19*th of April*, 1791."

Upon the 2nd of April, 1792, Mr. Wilberforce again brought the question of the slave-trade before the House of Commons, in a debate which did not end till near seven o'clock the next morning. It was ably supported by Mr. William Smith, Mr. Fox, Mr. Pitt and others on both sides of the House, irrespectively of party or politics. Mr. Pitt took a decided part in favour of its *immediate abolition*. Although he did not rise till a very late period of the debate, he spoke with great energy, exhausting all the stores of his mind, and all the powers of his eloquence to induce the House to concur with him in his opinion of the question.* This speech is de-

---

* This is the speech so highly and justly lauded by Mr. Fox in a subsequent debate. See p. 145, *note*.

scribed by Mr. Wilberforce as delivered by Mr. Pitt,* "with more energy and ability, than were almost ever exerted in the House of Commons. Windham, who has no love for Pitt, tells me that Fox and Grey, with whom he walked home after the debate, 'agreed with him in thinking Pitt's speech one of the most extraordinary displays of eloquence they ever heard. For the last twenty minutes he really seemed to be inspired.' He was dilating," continues Mr. Wilberforce, "upon the future prospects of civilizing Africa, a topic which I had suggested to him in the morning."

Mr. Dundas's motion for abolishing the trade *gradually*, instead of *immediately*, was carried by a majority of 238 to 85. On the 23rd of April, Mr. Dundas brought forward his motion for a gradual abolition, without naming any period. It was generally suspected that, if Dundas were forced to it, he would not name any specific time, but hold out the

---

* See *Life of Wilberforce*, by his Sons, p. 154.

prospect of an accelerated or retarded abolition, accordingly as the West India planters should more or less cordially agree with his plan; but he professed that if they did not concur, he would consent to immediate abolition. Neither Mr. Wilberforce nor his party credited Dundas's sincerity, and took measures accordingly; and after some debate, Lord Mornington's motion, which was supported and seconded by Mr. Pitt, for fixing the period of its abolition, on the 1st of January, 1795, was rejected by a majority of 161 to 121; and Sir Edward Knatchbull's motion for fixing it on the 1st of January, 1796, was subsequently carried by a majority of 151 to 132.

Mr. Wilberforce confessed that this degree of success was greater than he expected, and says,* " After a hard struggle we were, last night, defeated in our attempt to fix the period for the abolition for the 1st of January, 1795, Mr. Dundas had proposed

---

* *Life of Wilberforce*, by his Sons, p. 155.

1800; but we carried the first of January, 1796."
Dean Milner, the staunch friend of Wilberforce and
humanity, congratulated him on this first gain, and
concluded an affectionate, consolatory and stimulating
missive, on his past hopes and present fears, by saying,* "However, you have great reason to be
thankful, for GOD seems to bless your labours; and
I remember, that I told you long ago, that if you
carry this point in your whole life, that life will be
far better spent than in being prime minister for
many years."

Upon the 1st of May, when the question came
again before the House of Commons, Mr. Dundas
declared himself to be unable to propose his resolutions as amended by the late division. They were
therefore moved by Mr. Pitt, and on the following
day communicated to the House of Lords, in a free
conference. There the opponents of the measure
rallied their broken forces; and, in spite of Lord

---

* *Ibid.*

Grenville's able arguments, prevailed upon their lordships to proceed by calling evidence to their own bar; a resolution that was equivalent to the direct vote which followed it, on the 5th of June, that the further enquiry be postponed till the next session·

After these resolutions of the House of Commons had passed, the virtuous indignation of the country, which had been so strongly expressed in their petitions to parliament, having found vent, subsided into comparative indifference. The insurrections in St. Domingo, brought on by the increased cruelties of the republican government in Paris, the pretended advocates of liberty, equality and the rights of man, whose wild murderous course the negroes did but imitate, were rapturously seized upon by the partizans of slavery, and caused real fears among the friends of abolition, as to the example thus furnished to our African slaves in the other West India Islands. Jacobin,* republican, leveller, dividers of the wealth

---

* " Your friend, Mr. Wilberforce, will be happy to hand your

of the rich among the mob, demagogue, democrat, were but among the words hurled at the heads of Messrs. Wilberforce, Granville Sharp and their Quaker supporters. Mr. Pitt found enough to do with the war which he had just begun, opposed as he was by Fox and his powerful party, by his friend and companion Wilberforce, by a large portion of the country, and by the increasing disaffection of the labouring classes and lower orders of the people, to law, order, religion and government, as constituted in these kingdoms.

Although Mr. Wilberforce supported the Government, whenever he was able, the king and the royal family* showed their earnest displeasure at

---

ladyship to the guillotine," said Mr. Windham to the Countess Spencer. *Life of Wilberforce,* by his Sons, p. 184.

\* The Duke of Clarence took a prominent part in this business, (see the parliamentary debates of the day,) for which the corporation of Liverpool voted a splendid whole-length portrait of his royal highness in testimony of his services. It still adorns their town-hall, and is so excellent that it will be esteemed as a work of art when the subject will be forgotten.

R

his conduct. His filial biographers* record, " There had been a time when George III. had whispered at the levee, ' How go on your black clients, Mr. Wilberforce ?' but henceforth he was a determined opposer of the cause." And in another part of the work† last quoted, when Lord Grenville faltered in his place, and said, if the limitation of one slave to each one ton of the ship's‡ measurement were insisted upon, he would no longer fight their battle, " but would frankly declare he thought it ' an excess of zeal.' Now I am sure," continues this consistent, zealous and persevering philanthropist, " such an avowal from him, or any coldness on his part, would do us infinite mischief; for we have nothing to depend on against *the effect of St. James's and the Guelph family's being against us*, but that of Pitt and all his connexions and well known supporters being with us."

---

\* *Life*, p. 153.

† *Life of Wilberforce*, by his Sons, p. 156.

‡ According to Sir William Dolben's excellent Act.

On the 7th of February, 1793, Mr. Wilberforce moved for leave to bring in a bill to suppress the foreign slave-trade, which left unrestricted the supply to our own islands, and could not impede their cultivation, yet the whole force of the West India interest was arrayed against it. With great personal labour Mr. Wilberforce carried the bill through the House of Commons, after four divisions upon its three readings and its recommitment. In the House of Lords, it was abandoned by its former supporters to the assaults of the Duke of Clarence, Lord Abingdon and other opponents of humanity, and the second reading postponed till that day three months; by which vote the bill was rejected. On the 10th of the following March, Bishop Horsley made a motion in the House of Lords, to refer to a select committee the examination of witnesses upon the general question of abolition, which was then proceeding with leaden steps, at their lordships' bar; but it was rejected. In that House the business was continually procrastinated; and it was not till four days after the rejection of the bill sent up to them from the Commons that they summoned a single witness to their bar. Two witnesses was the modicum of their investigation, and then they let the subject drop.

On the 25th of March, 1795, the slave-trade abolition was again brought before the House of Commons, and although Mr. Wilberforce spoke long and eloquently, it was lost on a division of 78 to 61.

On the 15th of May, 1797, Mr. Wilberforce brought forward another motion in the House of Commons for the abolition of the slave-trade, and its opponents maintained the vantage ground they had previously obtained. Mr. Bryan Edwards,* who had just returned from Jamaica, and taken his seat in the House of Commons, ridiculed Mr.

---

* This gentleman, the historian of the West Indies, was born at Westbury, Wilts, in 1743, was educated in Bristol, and brought up in Jamaica by an uncle, from whom and a Mr. Hume, of that island, he inherited two large fortunes. He returned to England, and took his seat for the Cornish borough of Grampound, which he held to his death in 1800.

Wilberforce for declaring that by the gloomy aspect of public affairs, he was reminded of the slumbering wrath of heaven which the slave-trade must provoke; and taunted him with the humanity of the Liverpool merchants and the distresses of the chimney-sweepers. The motion was lost by a majority of 82 to 74.

Early in the spring of 1798 he again brought forward the abolition question before the House of Commons; and although Fox, Grey, Sheridan and other supporters attended, he was again defeated, against his expectations,* by the small majority of 87 to 83. The debate was long and earnest, and the West Indian majority was increased by the apparent concessions of its wily advocates. Encouraged by this diminution in the majority, a motion for the immediate abolition of the trade along the northern coast of Africa was brought forward by Mr. Henry Thornton, but the session was too far advanced, and

---

* "Thought we had carried it."—Diary in *Life of Wilberforce,* by his Sons, p. 339.

the House too full of business,*—the mutiny at Portsmouth, the income-tax, war with France, etc., for its consideration; and on the 18th of June it was deferred until the following session.

In 1799, the campaign against the slave-trade was re-opened by Mr. Wilberforce, who, on the 1st of March, brought forward a motion in the House of Commons for its immediate abolition. The sameness of a contest which had lasted for eleven years was enlivened by the wit and sarcasms of Mr. Canning, and relieved by the ever-varying eloquence of Pitt and Wilberforce. In this new effort he was again defeated but not dismayed, by 84 noes against 54 ayes. Two other measures of the preceding year were therefore revived : one, for regulating the middle passage, as it was technically called, was moved by Mr. William Smith and carried ; the other, for confining the trade within certain limits upon the coast of Africa, was moved, on the 5th of March,

---

* *Ibid.*, p. 239.

by Mr. Henry Thornton. On the second reading of this latter bill, " Pitt coolly put off the debate when I had manifested a desire of answering P.'s speech, and so left misrepresentation without a word."* On the 15th, Mr. Wilberforce attended the House, but was taken ill and forced home, and was " shocked," he says in his diary,† " to see Pitt and all the rest opposing the bill for limiting from part of the African coast, like entire abolition, alas !"

" Nothing," continues Mr. Wilberforce, " could exceed the earnestness with which Lord Grenville defended the Limitation Bill in the House of Lords. Unsupported by the immediate adherents of Government, he was left to withstand the repeated opposition of one member of the royal family,‡ the commercial sagacity of Lord Liverpool and the sturdy bluntness of Lord Thurlow : yet he was ready for every encounter, and maintained the conflict to the

---

* *Ibid.*, p. 253.     † *Ibid.*, p. 253.
‡ The Duke of Clarence.

last." While this bill was passing slowly through its different stages in the House of Lords, the friends of the abolition were preparing for a fresh encounter; and Parliament was prorogued, without further progress in the slave-trade question, on the 12th of July.

No steps towards the abolition question were taken in Parliament during the session of 1800, because "the West Indians had talked of a compromise," by which Mr. Wilberforce "hoped to be able to obtain a suspension of the slave-trade for five or seven years."* But, after much negociation, he was disappointed, and considered that "Pitt listened too easily to the assurances of several of the principal of the West Indian proprietors, who declared themselves willing to support a suspension for five years."

Lord Grenville proposed laying a tax upon all fresh imported negroes; but as slaves had risen in

---

* *Ibid.*, p. 265.

price from £76 to £120 per head, in spite of larger importations than ever, such a tax would be of no avail in diminishing the importations. Mr. Pitt, therefore, told Mr. Wilberforce,* that he would, by an order of council, stop the importation of negroes into the new settlements, into which three-fourths of the whole importation had been carried.

Peace having been made with France in 1802, suggested to the minds of the promoters of the abolition the formation of a grand European combination for that purpose; and, accordingly, Mr. Wilberforce deferred bringing it forward before the existing House of Commons, from which he had no hopes. But he redoubled his exertions in private with the Government. He learned from M. Otto, the French minister at our Court,† "that if our Government would propose to negociate for the immediate and total abolition, theirs would probably consent to it." The dangerous state of all the West India

---

* *Ibid.*, p. 266.          † *Ibid.*, p. 276.

islands, both British and foreign, alike aided and injured the scheme.

If Mr. Pitt had been in power, the negociation would have been tried, but Lord Hawkesbury and Mr. Addington would not undertake it. Mr. Wilberforce used all his endeavours to induce those ministers to negociate for a general abolition, but in vain. So that at last he wrote to each of them very serious letters, holding them to the responsibility. He was so dissatisfied with their conduct in the business that he declined an invitation to dine at M. Otto's to meet Mr. Addington and other members of the Government.

Mr. Canning's promised motion had been repeatedly deferred, and was again postponed, from the adverse temper displayed by the House; and Mr. Addington reluctantly engaged to pause before he opened the islands of St. Vincent and Trinidad for the reception of *another million of Africans*, during the fierce conflicts and insurrections of St. Domingo, Dominica and Tobago. He, nevertheless, made another effort on the 3rd of June, at a late hour and to a nearly empty house; and on the 14th abandoned it for that year, with better hopes for the next, as a dissolution of Parliament was at hand.

The hopes of the abolitionists were raised, by the return of Mr. Pitt to power on the 26th of April, 1804; and on the 30th of May, Mr. Wilberforce moved the first reading of his Abolition Bill, and carried it by a majority of 124 against 49. The bill was read a second time on the 7th of June. Lord Castlereagh spoke long and ably in its favour; Mr. Windham against it: Mr. Wilberforce replied briefly, and it was carried by 102 to 44. On the 12th the bill passed the committee: on the 25th, Mr. Pitt, in another eloquent speech in its favour, moved against hearing counsel or evidence, which he carried without a division; and on the 27th it was read a third time, and carried by a majority of 99 to 33.

Thus was the abolition of the slave-trade carried for a third time by the House of Commons.

Mr. Wilberforce, as the mover of the bill, had the honour of carrying it up to the House of Lords. On reaching that House, Bishop Porteus informed him* that he greatly feared for the success of the bill in the Lords, owing to the advanced period of the session, the probable sentiments of several noble lords in administration, and from the absence of by far the greater number of bishops at their dioceses. The bishop feared, also, that if it were to be rejected then, it would greatly injure the cause and impede its success another year. He therefore, by the advice of Mr. Pitt and Lord Grenville, suffered it to be suspended for another session, not without fears of insurrections in the West Indies or other events that would be turned against the cause of abolition.

In spite of the successful issue of the bill in the Commons, the withdrawing it from the Lords gave the friends of abolition the necessity of beginning their work again. Mr. Pitt, finding his majorities

---

* *Ibid.*, p. 317.

in Parliament much reduced by the secession of Lord Sidmouth and his friends, wished not to divide it by the introduction of the Abolition Bill during that session: Mr. Wilberforce, notwithstanding the earnest entreaties of the premier, being convinced by former experience that he must begin at once if he meant to carry it through both houses that session,* resolved to proceed.

Therefore, on the 6th of February, 1805, Mr. Wilberforce gave notice of his motion. " Pitt," he says,† "called upon me and was very kind about it." The bill was read a first time on the 19th, and the second reading fixed for the following week. On the third reading he replied briefly at the close of the debate, but was defeated by a slender majority of 77 against 70. Beaten but not disgraced, humbled yet exalted, he sought communion with his active out-door friends, and prepared zealously and fearlessly for a new campaign.

---

* 1804. See p. 251.
† *Life of Wilberforce*, by his Sons, p. 322.

In the interim William Pitt died,* "killed by the enemy as much as Nelson."

This national calamity dissolved the Government, and placed it in the hands of Lord Grenville, Lord Henry Petty, Mr. Fox, etc., all "good men and true" to the great cause of slave-trade abolition. Mr. Wilberforce records several interesting conferences with the leading members of the new cabinet, and his firm belief in their sincerity, notwithstanding their desire† " not to forfeit the Prince of Wales's favour, and that of G. R., and other anti-abolitionists."

After many conferences with the leading abolitionists, Mr. Wilberforce determined that a bill for the abolition of the foreign slave-trade should precede his general measure; and it was judged right to intrust it to one of the law-officers of the Crown. The Attorney-General (Sir Arthur Pigott) accordingly gave notice, in the House of Commons, of his

---

* *Ibid.*, p. 330.     † *Ibid.*, p. 333.

intention to bring in the Foreign Slave Bill. During the progress of this preliminary bill through the Commons, a similar one was introduced in the Lords by Lord Grenville, where it was carried triumphantly on the 10th of May.

This success was intended to have been followed up by the general bill; but, after conferences with Mr. Fox at Lord Grenville's and with his private friends and coadjutors, it was considered to be expedient to defer the general measure till the next session, and to propose a general resolution for abolition in both Houses of Parliament.

The object of the Foreign Slave-trade Bill, which had just then been passed in the Commons, was threefold. *First;* to give effect to the order of council which had been issued* at the close of the last year, which prohibited, with certain defined exceptions, the importation of slaves into the colonies conquered by the British arms during that war.

---

* See back, p. 231.

*Second;* to prohibit British subjects from being engaged in importing slaves into the colonies of any foreign power, whether hostile or neutral. *Third;* to prohibit British subjects and British capital from being employed in carrying on, or assisting to carry on, a slave-trade in foreign ships; and also to prevent the outfit of foreign slave-ships from British ports. An order of council subsequently extended the prohibition of that Act to the recently-captured colony of Buenos Ayres.

During the discussions to which this measure gave rise, both Lord Grenville and Mr. Fox declared* in substance, that they felt the question of the slave-trade to be one which involved the dearest interests of humanity, and the most urgent claims of policy, justice and religion; and that, should they succeed in effecting its abolition, they would regard that success as entailing more true glory on their administration, and more honour and advantage on their

---

* See Parliamentary Reports of that Session.

country, than any other transaction in which they could be engaged.

It had been, for the reasons before mentioned, considered expedient that the Foreign Slave-trade Bill should precede that for a total abolition; and, although it had passed the lower House, the session was too far advanced to hope it would pass into a law; it seemed to be highly desirable that both Houses of Parliament should, if possible, be prevailed on to admit and avow those sacred principles on which the propriety of the total abolition of that traffic was founded: principles indeed, which the House of Commons had long since openly acknowledged, but respecting which the House of Lords had not declared any opinion. Therefore it was desirable that both Houses should give a solemn pledge to the nation that they would proceed, without any unnecessary delay, to the investigation of the great practical questions which remained to be decided. A resolution was moved, on the 10th of June, 1806, by Mr. Fox in the House of Commons,

s

and by Lord Grenville, on the 24th of the same month, in the House of Lords, after receiving it from the Commons desiring their Lordships' concurrence thereto, to the following effect : " *That, conceiving the African slave-trade to be contrary to the principles of justice, humanity, and sound policy, this House will, with all practicable expedition, take measures to abolish it, in such manner, and at such time, as shall be thought advisable.*"

This motion gave rise to the debates, delineated in the history of which this monograph is but a fragment. In the House of Commons it was carried by a majority of 114 to 15, and in the House of Lords by 41 to 20.

Both Houses concurred in an Address to the King, praying his Majesty that he would be graciously pleased to negociate with foreign powers, for the purpose of procuring their concurrence in effecting a general abolition of the African slave-trade.

The orators in the House of Commons who spoke in this great debate were the following; and delivered their opinions in the following order; namely, Mr. SECRETARY FOX, who opened and closed the debate; Sir RALPH MILBANK, who seconded Mr. Fox's motion; General Tarleton; Mr. (afterwards Sir Philip) FRANCIS; Lord Castlereagh; the SOLICITOR-GENERAL (Sir Samuel Romilly); General Gascoigne; Mr. WILBERFORCE, who, after the division, in a neat and brief, but eloquent speech, moved the Address to the King, which was carried without a division; Sir William Young; Lord HENRY PETTY (the present Marquis of Lansdowne); Mr. Rose; Mr. Barham; Sir JOHN NEWPORT, who declared, in the course of his speech, that whatever difference of opinion might subsist in this part of the United Kingdom, on the question then before the House, in that part of it to which he had the honour to belong,* *there was but one universal abhorrence* of the African slave-trade, and an ardent desire to wipe off, as

---

* Ireland. The Right Hon. Baronet was the respected member for the city of Waterford, both in the Irish and Imperial Parliaments.

speedily as possible, the stain it had cast upon the character of the British nation. He alluded strongly to the interest they had in the trade, from their connection with Liverpool, Bristol, &c., and to the address in which that interest had been pressed upon their notice. But their answer was, said the Right Hon. Baronet, "We will have no share in a traffic consisting in rapine, blood and murder!" Honour be to Ireland! The member for Waterford was followed by Mr. CANNING, in a brief, but effective speech; Mr. Manning; Mr. WILLIAM SMITH, and Mr. Secretary* Windham. The names printed in small capitals were in favour of the motion, and the others against it.

The speakers in the House of Lords were—The Earl of Westmoreland, who endeavoured to retard the business, by proposing that counsel and evidence should be heard at the bar upon the subject about to be brought before the House, and *against the resolu-*

---

* See back, p. 139 (note), where this distinguished politician held opposite opinions.

*tion brought up* from the House of Commons; Lord
GRENVILLE, who opened and closed the debate; Lord
Hawkesbury (afterwards Earl of Liverpool); the
Bishop of LONDON (Dr. Porteus); the LORD CHAN-
CELLOR (Erskine);* the Bishop of ST. ASAPH (Dr.
Horsley): the Earl of SUFFOLK; Lord HOLLAND;
Lord Viscount Sidmouth; Earl STANHOPE; the Earl
of GROSVENOR; Earl Fitzwilliam; Lord ELLEN-
BOROUGH, and Earl SPENCER.

On the 15th of September, after this auspicious
triumph, Charles James Fox died also. Let the
following cantlet from his last speech serve for his
epitaph :—

" I do confess, that since I have sat in this House,
a period of between thirty and forty years, if I had
done nothing else, but had only been instrumental in
carrying through this measure, I should think my
life well spent, and should retire quite satisfied that
I had not lived in vain."

---

* See back, p. 122, latter part of note.

Lord Thurlow, a bitter enemy, and Bishop Horsley, a sincere friend to the cause, both took their departure from this scene of strife for regions of greater peace and concord in the same momentous year.

The death of Mr. Fox caused a dissolution of the Parliament that had so triumphantly carried his resolution. Mr. Wilberforce was again returned as one of the members for Yorkshire, and in concert with Lord Grenville and the ministry and his little senate, he prepared to begin the campaign vigorously. He wrote and issued a stirring pamphlet on the subject, which he circulated among the members of both Houses with effect. Mr. Roscoe said, in a letter,[*] that "its beneficial effects could not escape the observation of any one who attended the discussion in the Lords."

On Friday, the 22nd of January, 1807, Lord Grenville opened the attack, by presenting to the

---

* *Life of Wilberforce*, by his Sons, p. 340.

House of Lords a bill, entitled "A Bill for the abolition of the Slave-trade," which was read a first time. His lordship then moved, that the bill be printed and lie upon the table a sufficient time for mature consideration previous to its discussion, and would therefore not fix any day at present for the second reading. The Duke of Clarence, Lord Eldon, and Lord Hawkesbury said a few words, indicative of their intention to oppose the bill in its future stages, and the motion was agreed to.

On Wednesday, the 4th of February, the day fixed for the second reading of the bill, the order to that effect was read; when it was resolved, that the petitioners against the bill should be heard by their counsel. The petitioners were the Liverpool merchants, the town and corporation of Liverpool, the West India planters and merchants, and the planters and merchants of Trinidad. Each of the learned counsel proposed to call witnesses in proof of their case. The House negatived the proposition, and counsel were then heard. This process having occupied the House to a late hour, the second reading of the bill was accordingly deferred to the following day.

That day having arrived, the order of the day having been read, the grand debate began, this time in the Lords by Lord Grenville; and, after the same preliminary hearing of counsel, in the Commons, by Lord Howick, on Tuesday, the 10th of February, 1807. After long and interesting debates, which are referred to the history, the bill was carried in the House of Lords, at four o'clock in the morning, by a majority of 72 contents and 28 proxies = 100, against 28 not contents and 8 proxies = 36; and in the House of Commons by a majority of 283 to 16.

The speakers in the House of Lords were—Lord GRENVILLE ;* the Duke of Clarence, who followed Lord Grenville's long, argumentative and statesman-like view of the subject, by opposing it on the

---

* The *pros* and *cons* are indicated as in the last list.

ground of the injury which must result from the measure to the commerce and naval power of this country, and predicted that it "would not be abolished." Alas for Royal foresight! The Duke of GLOUCESTER next addressed the House, in a speech worthy of a descendant of the House of Brunswick, successfully combatted the assertions of his Royal kinsman, and affirmed "the trade in question to be a cruel and criminal traffic in the blood of our fellow-creatures, and therefore a foul stain on the national character, and an offence to the Almighty." The Earl of Westmoreland, who entered into a long defence of the slave-trade, and endeavoured to deaden the force of Lord Grenville's arguments; the Earl of SELKIRK; Viscount Sidmouth; the Earl of ROSSLYN, who in a very luminous speech, replied to Lord Sidmouth's objections and claimed the noble Viscount's support, on his own principles. Lord Rosslyn's speech was throughout replete with solid argument and convincing statements. Earl St. Vincent, who asserted, among other things, that he* "was fully persuaded, from personal observation, that *the planters in our islands were the most humane set of men, and the negroes the happiest set of beings in the universe!*" Lord HOOD, who from similar observation deduced directly opposite conclusions from the last speaker. "He was not," he said, "like the noble Earl, living on board his ship, and paying only occasional visits to the plantations, but residing for long periods of time, on one occasion for two years, on shore. He had seen such a mass of misery on those islands, that *he could not satisfy his conscience not to come and give all the support of which he was capable to this grand measure of justice and benevolence.*" He then related several facts which had passed under his own observation, as proving the wretched, helpless and degraded state of the negro slaves. The House was visibly affected by the noble Admiral's relation. Lord KING; Lord

---

* This gallant admiral was too well known in the Royal Navy by the *sobriquet* of "Flogging Jervis."

Eldon; the Bishop of DURHAM; Earl MOIRA, who had told* Mr. William Smith to confer with the Prince of Wales, and was therefore supposed to represent his Royal Highness's altered opinions, made a masterly and dignified appeal to the justice and feeling of the House. Lord Hawkesbury, who repeated his former arguments in vindication of the trade, although he admitted it to be *a great evil*. Lord HOLLAND, who replied to the last speaker and to others who had defended the slave-trade, in an eloquent and impressive speech. But when towards its close he alluded to Mr. Fox, he was overpowered, and there were few in the House who did not appear to sympathize with him.

On the 6th of February the House went into a committee on the bill, and filled up the blanks; on the 9th, the report of the committee was received; and on the 10th the bill was read a third time, and sent to the Commons; on which day it was read a

---

* *Life of Wilberforce*, by his Sons, p. 333.

first time, ordered to be read a second time on the 20th when counsel were heard, and the grand debate took place on the 23rd, with the result before mentioned.

The speakers on this occasion in the House of Commons, and the order in which they rose, were, after a conversation between Mr. Manning and Lord Howick on the subject of compensation,—Lord HOWICK, who opened the debate; General Gascoigne;* Mr. ROSCOE;† Mr. LUSHINGTON; Mr. WALTER FAWKES, Mr. Wilberforce's new colleague for the county York; Lord MAHON; Lord MILTON; Mr. BATHURST; Sir JOHN DOYLE;‡ Sir SAMUEL ROMILLY, who in the course of a brilliant and effective oration against slavery in general and the slave-trade in particular, and handling all the objections made against the bill with able dexterity, proving all his statements by incontrovertible facts, finished with the following exquisite peroration,

---

* See back, p. 212.     † *Ibid.*, p. 220.
‡ *Ibid.*, pp. 198 (note), 207, and 217—220.

which caused,* says Wilberforce, " the whole House, surprised into a forgetfulness of its ordinary habits, to burst forth into acclamations of applause." Addressing himself to the House in general, as to the consolation their successors would feel in remembering that their forefathers were those who first put an end to that abominable trade, he alluded to the younger members, who might live to witness all those benefits, to whom it was reserved, perhaps, the greatest happiness which in this state of existence man is permitted to enjoy. " What a delightful reflection," he exclaimed, "is it to think, that generations yet unborn will bless our memories, as the authors of their liberty and happiness." "But, Sir," said our great forensic orator, " if such will be the feelings of those who have borne any part in this transaction, or who have even witnessed its completion, what must be the feelings of my† honourable friend? What is there in the wide

---

* *Life*, p. 341.          † Mr. Wilberforce.

range of human ambition, which could afford pleasure so pure, gratification so exalted, as he must
enjoy? When I look to the man who has placed on
his brow the imperial diadem of France, surrounded
with all the pomp of power, and all the pride of
victory, dethroning and creating monarchs at his
will, distributing kingdoms to his family, and princi-
palities to his favourites,—seeming, when he sits
upon his throne, with his prostrate kings and princes
paying him their servile homage, to have reached
the summit of human ambition, and the pinnacle of
earthly happiness: and when I survey the inmost
recesses of that man's mind,—when I follow him
into his closet or to his bed, and consider the pangs
with which *his* solitude must be tormented, and his
repose disturbed, as he recollects the blood he has
shed, the devastation and misery he has occasioned,
and the amount of human happiness he has destroyed. And when, turning from this disgusting
spectacle, I compare with his pangs of remorse the
feelings which must accompany my honourable

friend from this House to his own, after the vote of this night shall have accomplished the object of his humane and unceasing labours; the feelings, I say, which must swell the bosom of my honoured friend, when retiring from this roof to the domestic circle of his happy family, he reposes his head upon his pillow, and reflects on the prayers that will be offered up to heaven for his protection, I must regard *him* as an object of just envy to the most ambitious of mortals. Who will not be proud to concur with him in promoting the greatest act of national benefit, and securing to the Africans the greatest blessing which GOD has ever put it in the power of man to confer upon his fellow-creatures." After the sensation had subsided, Mr. Hibbert spoke long and loudly against the bill; Mr. WILBERFORCE for it; Mr. Manning, amidst clamours of "Question, question, question," against it; and Mr. HILEY ADDINGTON, amidst still louder calls of "Question," in its support. Lord PERCY, amidst increased clamours, supported the bill, and the House divided with the result stated.

On Friday, the 27th of February, 1807, the
House, on the motion of Lord Howick, resolved itself
into a committee on the bill; and on the question
being put for the Speaker to leave the chair, Sir
Charles Pole declared his intention to oppose it in
all its stages; Mr. WYNNE supported it; Mr. Hughan
and Mr. Brown against; Mr. BARHAM reluctantly
for it, with compensation; Mr. COURTNEY for the
bill; Sir RALPH MILBANK for; Mr. MONTAGUE, who
spoke well in its favour; Mr. BATHURST; Mr.
JACOB; Mr. Windham; Mr. WHITBREAD, who
wished with all his heart that his excellent friend,
Mr. William Smith, who had so long and zealously
laboured in this noble cause, had then been a member
of that assembly, that he might have had the gratification of co-operating in that great work; and
" I thank God," said Mr. Whitbread, " that I have
lived to this day, when I can give my vote for
abolishing this nefarious traffic, in the assured hope
that the period of its extinction has at length
arrived." The other members who addressed the

House were Mr. Fuller; Mr. HERBERT, of Kerry; and Lord HOWICK, who, after a brief and able refutation of Mr. Windham and other opponents, again moved for the Speaker to leave the chair, which being agreed to, the House immediately went into committee, Mr. HOBHOUSE in the chair. The bill then went, *pro formâ*, through the committee, the House resumed, the report was received and read; it was resolved that the bill be taken into further consideration on a future day, and that it be printed as amended.

On Friday, March 6th, 1807, on the motion of Lord Howick, the House resolved itself into a committee, Mr. HOBHOUSE in the chair. The speakers were—Sir Charles Pole, who concluded with moving that the date 1812 be substituted for 1807; Mr. WARD; Sir PHILIP FRANÇIS, who had sat, he said, in that House for nearly thirty years, had listened, during that time, to all the debates on that important subject, which had been discussed there for twenty years, and "forsooth we are now to be told

T

of hurry and precipitation. After twenty years, to avoid what is called *impolitic haste*, we are to give five more years to the trade!" General VYSE, who considered that on the result of the question before the House depended *the eternal happiness or misery of England*, and he could not tell how those who opposed the bill could satisfy their consciences in shutting the gates of mercy on mankind. Sir THOMAS TURTON; Mr. HILEY ADDINGTON, with a wish, however, to defer the abolition till 1812; Mr. WHITBREAD; Mr. ROSE; Lord HENRY PETTY; Mr. CANNING, who concluded an eloquent speech by declaring, that it would be a consolation to him that the planters would find that their interest, when it is largely considered, was on the same side as humanity to mankind and to the world. Mr. STANHOPE; Mr. BATHURST, but for the longest period. Mr. PERCEVAL, who would reject the bill if clogged with the delay of five years: he would propose it from year to year till successful, which he felt assured would be long before the proposed extension.

The question was then put on Sir Charles Pole's amendment, that 1812 be substituted for 1807; when, after some explanations between Mr. Wilberforce and Mr. Fuller, a division took place, when the numbers for the amendment were 17, and against it 125, majority 108. The chairman, Mr. HOBHOUSE, then read the bill, paragraph by paragraph; when, after a few words from Mr. Rose, Sir Charles Pole and Lord Howick, it was agreed that the chairman should report the bill with the amendments to the House on Monday.

On that day, the 16th of March, on the motion of Lord Henry Petty, the question was put from the chair, that "The bill for the abolition of the slave-trade, be read a third time?" The members who addressed the House on this final step were, Mr. Hibbert, one of those

" Cits who prefer a guinea to mankind,"*

who after reviving all the former arguments against the bill, closed his last speech, by saying, " If I have

* Granville.

said to-night what is rather the dictates of warmth and passion, than of reason and of truth, I shall be sorry for it to-morrow; and I hope the House, in its candour, will contemplate it, *as the last effort in favour of an expiring friend!*" Sir PHILIP FRANCIS, who indignantly repelled Mr. Hibbert's misrepresentation, that " he had said that all those who were partakers of this detestable traffic ought to be out of the protection of the law ;" denying at the same time the right of any member to allude to any speech made on a former debate. He denied it wholly, and repeated what he did say, which was a general proposition as to compensation for transactions, which the House had declared to be " contrary to justice, humanity, and sound policy. Mr. LITTLETON; Mr. HENRY THORNTON, a long and luminous exposition of the subject. Mr. Herbert ;* Mr. T. W. Plomer; Mr. Barham; Mr. Windham, who candidly acknow-

---

* Not the member for Kerry, see p. 273, who gave the bill his hearty support.

ledged that if the result of the measure should be
beneficial, he would confess that he had had no share
in promoting it; but if it should be followed by the
fearful consequences he apprehended, he should at
least be free from all culpability in having accelerated
those calamities.*    Mr. SHERIDAN, who replied successfully to Mr. Windham, and considered it to be
a disgrace to the British Parliament, that the measure had not been long before acceded to.    Lord
Castlereagh; and Mr. WILBERFORCE who eloquently
and fully replied to the objections made against the

---

* See Mr. Windham's former declarations as to slavery, p.
139 (note), and even in his speeches on this debate as reported.
Mr. Wilberforce (Life, p. 504,) accounts for this inconsistency.
" Windham's mind was in the last degree copious, the soil was
so fertile, scratch where you pleased up came white clover.
He had many of the true characteristics of a hero, but he had
one great fault as a statesman, he hated the popular side of any
question," said a mutual friend to Mr. Wilberforce, who, in
recording it in his diary, adds, " I had a melancholy proof of
this in the instance of the slave trade :  when our abolition had
but few friends, he was all on our side, but as the nation drew
towards us, he retreated; and at last on the division in 1807,
he was one of the sixteen who voted against us."

measure.   At the close of his speech, Mr. Wilberforce made some grateful allusions to several individuals, " who," he declared, " had done themselves
immortal honour, by their strenuous and persevering
exertions in this great cause," on all of whom he
pronounced appropriate eulogies.   Mr. Pitt and Mr.
Fox, Lord Grenville, the Bishop of London, Mr.
Granville Sharp, Mr. Clarkson, Mr. Roscoe, the
member for Liverpool, and the different members of
the Administration,  and other able and eloquent
supporters of the measure.   He concluded by con-
gratulating the House and the nation upon the adop-
tion of the bill ; which he regarded as one of the
greatest services that had been rendered to humanity,
and on the general principles which had been avowed
as the foundation of the proceeding.   He expressed
also his deep sense of the obligation under which
he, the House, and the kingdom at large, had been
laid, by the noble manner in which his Majesty's
ministers had acted with respect to this great measure.

The bill was then read a third time and passed; and it was ordered "that Mr. Wilberforce do carry it to the Lords."

On Monday, the 23rd of March, 1807, on the motion of Lord Grenville, the order of the day, for considering the amendments introduced by the House of Commons, into the "Bill for the abolition of the slave-trade," was read. After a speech from the Bishop of Llandaff,* in favour of the bill, and from the Earl of Westmoreland against it, and a few observations from the Marquis of Sligo, and the Duke of Norfolk, the several amendments were read and agreed to.

Lord Grenville then rose and said, "I now move your Lordships, that a message be sent to the Commons, to signify your assent to the amendments made by them. Permit me, my Lords, for the last time, to congratulate the House upon the completion of one of the most glorious tasks that was ever per-

---

* Dr. Richard Watson.

formed for the public benefit." The motion of Lord Grenville was carried *nem. con.* ; the message was sent to the Commons ; the bill received the royal assent, and became the law of the land.

The battle having been won, the victory having been gained, the veteran chiefs did not rest upon their arms, reposing under the glories of their oaken chaplets, as if their labours were at end, but sought, with the assistance of younger auxiliaries who had joined their ranks, to accomplish the work by seeing the provisions of the bill duly and honestly executed. Granville Sharp* was in his 74th year, but vigorous both in body and mind; Clarkson and Wilberforce, both born in the same year,† were in their 46th year, but the latter was feeble in body,§ arising from the effects of that disease which a few years

---

* This excellent man, of whom more is recorded in the history, died on the 13th of July, 1813, in his 80th year.

† 1759, as was also William Pitt.

§ Not long after that time, he wrote in his diary, "I am become heavy and lumbering, and not able at once to start into a canter, as I could twenty years ago."

before compelled him to surrender his command to Mr. Pitt, and had nearly terminated his earthly career.

To continue the goodly work, the original promoters of its sacred cause established trading companies to Sierra Leone and other parts of the African coast; established what Mr. Wilberforce called a congress, to which were added the younger and unfatigued colleagues, Henry Brougham, Thomas Fowell Buxton, Macaulay, Whitmore, etc.; Mr. Wilberforce began to prepare a manifesto before opening the ensuing parliamentary campaign; the congress were as indefatigable as ever in the laborious occupation of collecting and arranging details. Mr. Buxton, ardent for the fray, informed his leader that he should be in town by the 10th of January, 1808, and expressed his hope that the congress on the subject would not be later; to which the sagacious commander replied,* "It is exceedingly well

---

* *Life of Wilberforce*, by his Sons, p. 505.

for you, who have powder and ball, that is, knowledge of the whole subject, and the power of projecting it with force, to be primed and loaded of a morning and fired off at night, but it will not do with me, I can do nothing in this rapid method." The object of the congress was now to call on all the good men throughout the kingdom to join them in abolishing the wicked system of slavery, and to render the degraded race of negroes a free peasantry, by ameliorating their condition, as a prelude to emancipation.

Parliament met in February, 1823, and early in March the manifesto or appeal was published. It was much approved and produced great effect. Its perusal so much affected a West Indian proprietor, that he told Mr. Wilberforce, " that should it cost him his whole property, he would willingly surrender it, that his poor negroes might be brought, not only to the liberty of Europeans, but, especially, to the liberty of Christians."*

---

* *Ibid.*, p. 508.

On the 19th of March, 1823, Mr. Wilberforce presented to the House of Commons, a petition from the Society of Friends, reproachfully called Quakers, in favour of amelioration and religious instruction, cultivating marriage and other means of improving the condition of the African slaves in our West India Colonies, to prepare them for the blessings of emancipation.* His object was to bring the subject prominently forward, to ascertain the temper of the House, and to prepare such ulterior measures as it would bear. He, therefore, moved that the petition be received, be printed, &c., which were carried. But the cold question of Canning, who was then Foreign Secretary in the Perceval cabinet, whether the honourable member intended to make a distinct motion, dumbfounded the leader and closed the lips of all the friends of the cause. They were all of them as he says, " *abattus.*"†

---

* This petition came with singular propriety from this body, which having been the first to lift up their voice against the slave-trade, now raised it again against slavery.

† *Ibid.*, p. 508.

Mr. Buxton, to whom had now been committed the leadership in the great work of African freedom, took up the subject on the 15th of May, and moved a resolution declaring slavery repugnant to Christianity and to the British constitution. Mr. Canning replied, and moved a series of resolutions promising a reform of the system, and specifying, driving, punishment of females, Sunday work, and markets as among the grievances. This placed the friends to the cause in an awkward dilemma, and there the case rested. On the 4th of July, the slave-trade consolidation bill, which was intended to prevent exportation of slaves to Trinidad was brought forward in the House of Commons, and lost. Mr. Hume was strongly against them and urged that the power of the Privy Council to grant licenses for removing slaves from island to island, not excluding Trinidad, should *be perpetual* and not confined to three years, as proposed by Mr. Wilmot Horton.

In the beginning of the Parliamentary session in February, 1824, Mr. Buxton, Mr. Brougham, Mr.

Wilberforce and other friends to the cause, were early and active in their exertions in the House; whilst "The African Association" laboured without doors. On the 14th, a deputation from that society waited upon Mr. Canning,* but were sadly disappointed by his plan of merely setting up the particulars he had consented to the preceding year, by an Order of Council in Trinidad  They were with the Foreign Secretary from 12 till 2, and then went to the Duke of Gloucester's, where they met the Marquis of Lansdowne, Mr. Brougham, Mr. Stephen and other friends to the cause, to arrange the mode of proceeding.

The debate on the resolutions came on on the 16th of February. Mr. Canning opened the discussion in a very cautious manner; Mr. Buxton succeeded the Minister in a strong energetic speech; Mr. Wilberforce continued the debate, in "better voice,"† he records, "and better heard than usual." He was "determined," he said, "to wash his hands

---

* *Ibid.*, p. 511.        † *Ibid.*, p. 513.

of the blood which might be spilled by thus trifling with the hopes of men." The ministerial measure was carried, and another step, although not a great one, was gained to the cause.

The next measure of the friends, was the case of Smith the Missionary, who had been imprisoned by the authorities of Demerara, after the outbreak of the negroes against their masters, for concealing the Order of Council, and had died in prison. The subject was brought before the House of Commons on the 1st of June. Mr. Brougham made an admirable speech upon the subject, which Mr. Wilberforce, who had left a sick bed for the first time for nearly nine weeks, to attend this duty, records as "Capital,"* and Sir James Mackintosh well termed "Impregnable." "Mackintosh's own," says Mr. Wilberforce, "was most beautiful, his mind teemed with ideas." The decision was postponed till the 11th. In the interval, he records in his diary, "I very much wish, if my voice should

---

* *Ibid.*, p. 514.

be strong enough, to bear testimony against the scandalous injustice exercised upon poor Smith. The case proved against him is greatly short of what I thought it might have been. I myself once saw a Missionary's Journal, and its contents would have been capable of being perverted into a much stronger charge of promoting discontent among the slaves. Had I happened, for instance, to have corresponded with Smith, that alone would have hanged him."

On the day of the adjourned debate, Mr. Wilberforce spoke, but with evident diminution of power; among the other speakers were Mr. Canning, Mr. Lushington, Mr. Denman, Mr. Williams and Mr. Brougham, who replied with singular eloquence and energy. The speech made by Mr. Wilberforce on this occasion was the last he ever delivered in the House of Commons. After declaring that his only hope for the manumission of the negroes, and the abolition of slavery was to be from the British Parliament alone, as the West Indians were opposed to all their humane measures, he concluded his Oration for Universal Liberty, with the following prophetic words,—" It is with reluctance and pain that I come forward, but I esteem it to be my bounden duty, to protest against the policy on which we are now acting. *'Liberavi animam meam.'* May it please GOD to disappoint my expectations, and to render the result more favourable than I anticipate."

In February, 1825, Mr. Wilberforce retired from Parliament, confirming Mr. Buxton in the Parliamentary heirship, to which he had named him two years before. Mr. Buxton, in his reply, happily reminded his venerated leader of the inscription which the Carthaginians placed upon the tomb of Hannibal :—

"WE VEHEMENTLY DESIRED HIM IN THE DAY OF BATTLE."

On the 21st of December following his retirement from Parliament, a great meeting of the Anti-slavery Society was held in Freemason's Hall, at which he was solicited to preside, and consented, with some reluctance, in consequence of bodily weakness arising from the serious illness, from which he had but recently recovered. He "got to the meeting at 12, took the chair, and was very kindly treated throughout, both by the full room and by the speakers."*

Another meeting of the Anti-slavery Society was held on the 15th of May, 1830, when Mr. Wilberforce, with a weakened voice and an enfeebled frame, consented to take the chair. All the old friends of the cause gathered around him, and Freemasons' Hall again overflowed with a zealous and attentive audience. This was the last time he took any part in London for the anti-slavery cause.

A general election followed this meeting, and one of its beneficial results was, that Mr. Brougham and three other candidates, pledged to slave emancipation, were returned representatives for the great and important County of York, which had ever led the way in this good cause.

---

* *Ibid.*, p. 526.

Although Mr. Wilberforce had attended an anti-slavery meeting in London for the last time, and had proposed to himself an absolute retirement from public life, yet his ardent zeal in the cause for which he had so long laboured, induced him, on the 12th of April, 1833, to propose at a meeting of the Free-holders of the County of Kent, held in the Town-hall of Maidstone, a petition to Parliament against slavery, to which he affixed his signature. At this meeting, Mr. Wilberforce made his last speech, with a clear though weakened voice, but with unimpaired judgment. Immediate emancipation was unquestioned, but the principle of compensation was disputed. He had proposed to Mr. Canning, ten years before, the formation of a fund to indemnify those persons who should be proved to have really suffered by a change in the West Indian system; previous compensation for anticipated injury being, in his opinion, the only way to postpone for ever all the improvements of the system. Against that measure he therefore all along contended, even while he admitted that Great Britain owed "smart-money" for her former encouragement of the slave-trade; and hailed with joy the proposed grant of *twenty millions sterling!* to purchase the manumission of all British slaves. In this last effort he declared, "I say, and say honestly and fearlessly, that the same BEING who commands us to love mercy, says also, 'do justice.'"

On that very day, whilst sitting at dinner with his Kentish friends, it was casually hinted to him, that probably at that moment the debate on the abolition of slavery was began: he sprung from his seat, and, with his clear voice, startled his surrounding friends, by suddenly exclaiming, in a most striking manner,* "Hear! hear! hear!" On that 12th of April, 1833, the Bill for the Abolition of Slavery was read the first time in the House of Commons; the second time, on the 26th of July,

---

* *Life*, by his Sons, p. 549.

and in a few days afterwards it became the law of the land.

The great fact was then accomplished. Clarkson and Wilberforce, the survivors of the glorious trio, (Granville Sharp then resting with his fathers,) who had begun, continued and ended the contest, witnessed its happy termination. The world then saw the heavily burdened, overtaxed people of these united kingdoms, purchasing the unlawful property, the slaves of its colonists, at a fair valuation, and instantly declaring them as free as themselves, and acknowledging them as fellow-subjects of the freest state upon earth.

Think of this, fellow Christians of the United States of America, and ask yourselves this question, Can the holders of fellow men as slaves, call their community a free state?

This great act of the legislature gave entire satisfaction to the whole nation. Corporations, societies and individuals voted thanks to its authors; the blessings of millions were wafted to heaven in their behalf; and our nation and people have risen from their previous calamities, and have increased from day to day, in public prosperity and importance, and in private virtue and happiness. The history of the intervening period, from the hour of passing the Act for the Abolition of Slavery to the present day, bears out my assertion.

The Corporation of London, always forward in honouring public virtue, on the 29th of November, 1838, " Resolved unanimously that the freedom of this city be presented to Thomas Clarkson, A.M., and that he be requested to sit for a marble bust, to be placed in this Court, as grateful testimonials of the corporation of London, to the public services and worth of one who had the merit of originating, and has the consolation of living to witness, the triumph of the great struggle for the deliverance of the enslaved African from the most oppressive bondage, that ever tried the endurance of afflicted humanity ; thereby obtaining for his country the high distinction of separating her commercial greatness from principles incompatible with the exercise of the religion of mercy, and achieving a moral victory, whose trophies shall endure while justice, freedom, the clemency of power and the peaceful glories of civilization shall have a place in the admiration of mankind."

The Court resolved also that the Right Hon. the Lord Mayor, (Sir Chapman Marshall,) be requested to give the necessary directions for carrying the foregoing resolution into effect. Mr. Behnes was accordingly commissioned to execute the bust;* an engraving from which, copied by permission of the late Lord Mayor, (Alderman Challis,) forms the frontispiece of this illustration of one of the passages of his long and useful life.

On the 29th of April, 1839, the Lord Mayor, (Sir Chapman Marshall,) reported to the Court of Common Council, that all matters connected with

---

* The bust cost 200 guineas, exclusive of the lofty pedestal upon which it is placed.

the execution of the marble bust of Mr. Clarkson, and the presentation of the freedom of the city to that distinguished philanthropist, pursuant to the resolution of that Court of the 29th of November, 1838, had been accomplished; and that Mr. Clarkson had been admitted to the freedom of the city, at the Mansion House, on Monday, the 15th day of April instant, at the request of the family of Mr. Clarkson on account of his advanced age.

It was then resolved,—"That the circumstances of the admission of Thomas Clarkson, A.M., to the freedom of this city, taking place at the Mansion House of the Lord Mayor, be not drawn into precedent."

The above resolution, so honourable to both parties, was written ornamentally on vellum, splendidly emblazoned with armorial bearings, trophies and appropriate emblems, and handsomely framed and glazed, was presented to Mr. Clarkson.

On the 12th of June, the great convention of the Anti-slavery Society was held at Freemasons' Hall.

A day or two before the meeting, a deputation waited upon my old and deeply lamented friend, Haydon, and said they wished him to make a sketch of the scene, probably for a picture. It was my intention to have attended, but official engagements in the lower part of the port of London prevented me· Haydon described it as most affecting; but its details belong to the larger history, to which this fragment is but a precursor.

This meeting was the last public assembly, I believe, that Mr. Clarkson attended, although not his last public act. There was also at this Congress of Freedom, delegates from America and other parts of the world. Haydon made his sketches, returned home, and, with his usual alacrity and rapidity, made one in oil colours. The next day, the painter "breakfasted with Mr. Clarkson,* and sketched him and his dear grandson as the most beautiful of the group." On the 15th he again breakfasted with Mr.

---

* See his *Autobiography*, Vol. iii., p. 141.

Clarkson, and made another and more aged sketch, though a friend said of the other, that it had the look of indignant humanity. The conversation between painters and sitters, vary with the persons so occupied. Think of those between Charles II., Eleanor Gwyn, Count Grammont, Lady Castlemaine, or any of the languishing beauties of that period, with the flattering Sir Peter Lely, and compare it with such as might occur between the truthful Reynolds and such sitters as Burke, Johnson, Bennet Langton, or the other distinguished characters whose souls he has depicted with his magic pencil. Such conversations may be imagined; but that between Haydon and Clarkson at this sitting, was entered, warm from the heart, by the painter, in his faithful diary, before the day had closed upon his labours.

Haydon said, "Mr. Clarkson, those who have a great national object, should be virtuous and see GOD daily, 'enduring, as seeing one who is invisible.'" "They do indeed," replied Mr. Clarkson, "it supported me; I have worked day and night,

and I have awoke in convulsions after reading the
evidence of the horrors of the slave-trade." Haydon
replied, " Christianity is the power of God unto
salvation. It is of heart and internal conviction,
not of evidence and external proof." " Ah!" said
Clarkson, " what a blessing is the religious feeling.
The natural man sees flowers and hears birds, and
is pleased; the religious man attributes all to GOD."

Portrait painters, above most persons who study
" the human face divine," see the spirit playing in
the countenance. Sir Joshua Reynolds would paint
no man of mark or likelihood till he had studied his
intellectual character, sparkling in the eye, speaking in the expanse of the brow, and darting indignation, contempt, gratification and other passions
expressed by the face, over the convivial board,
or the intellectual collision of the evening conversations: and Rosalba Carriera said she had " been so
long accustomed to study features, and the expression of the mind by them, that I know people's
tempers by their faces. In proof of this faculty,"

she added, says Spence,* "the characters of two of
my friends, whom she had seen but twice or thrice,
and my own, as justly, (and the last perhaps more
so,) as I could have done myself." The two portraits
thus sketched, caused Haydon, with similar feelings,
to record, in his diary, that Clarkson looked to him
"like a man whose nerves had been strained," and
observed to him at the close of the last sitting, " I
have a cause at my heart, though not of so much
interest to mankind as yours; I hope GOD will
bless it."

From this interesting sitting Haydon went to the
committee, and arranged to take four sitters the
next day. He went to the convention at 7,
breakfasted with them, and proceeded with his
drawings till 4. The following day saw him at
his post at the same hour, breakfasting and conversing with the committee, and continuing drawing

---

* *Observations, Anecdotes and Characters of Books and
Men.*

their heads till 4. " Made fourteen sketches of heads
in one day, till my brain got dazzled. I have made
thirty sketches in three days. Whilst I was sketch-
ing Mr. Scobell, M. Cordier, the French avocat,
came to arrange. He said, ' *Monsieur, est il néces-
sairé de venir dans mes regimentaux de Pair de
France?* ' " Haydon slily hints, " I ought to have
said, ' *Monsieur, vous n'avez pas emancipé les
esclaves ; mais les regimentaux de Pair de France
l'equivalent.* ' " " Good God !" writes the indignant painter, " in such a cause to think of his
costume as a ' *Pair de France !* ' " The other
French delegate, M. Crémeur, made an appointment
at his lodgings in Piccadilly, for 9 the next morning : Haydon drove up with his usual punctuality,
and the delegate was " not at home." Madame
came down *en deshabille,* and assured the impatient
artist " *Que Monsieur était sorti touchant les affaires
les plus important,—mais a dix heures, Monsieur.*"
Haydon took his leave. He continued his extraordinary mental and manual exertions till the 20th,

when he had completed fifty-five heads of the members of the convention in five days.

On the 30th Mr. Scobell called on the painter about the picture, and was told by him of his intention of placing him, Mr. Thompson, and the negro delegate together. Nothing can give a finer idea of American feeling touching their coloured brethren, *even when free*, than the colloquy which occurred between the painter and his sitter, as recorded by the former. "An abolitionist," he says, " on thorough principles would have gloried in being so placed. This was the touchstone. He sophisticated immediately on the greater propriety of placing the negro in the distance, as it would have a much greater effect. Now I, who have never troubled my head in the cause, gloried in the idea of placing the negro close by the side of his emancipator. The emancipator shrank. I'll do it though. Scobell," he adds, " is a fine fellow, but he and Tredgold felt a little touched at the idea. If he has suffered for the cause, why object?"

Lucretia Mott, the leader of the female delegates from America sat, and he had placed her in a prominent place in the picture, from which Haydon removed her on finding her to have infidel notions; and reserved it " for a beautiful believer in the divinity of Christ." Lloyd Garrison, another delegate, also sat, the painter asked him about the negro, and he met his views directly. George Thompson said, he saw no objection. This was not enough for the enthusiastic painter, who writes plainly in his diary that " a man who wishes to place the negro on a level with himself, must no longer regard him as having been a slave, and feel annoyed at sitting by his side." This is an *argumentum ad hominem*, which our white brethren across the Atlantic cannot brook.

On the 3rd of July he drew in the negro and the head of the delegate from Hayti, and sketched Lady Byron and Lucretia Mott. With Lady Byron, he was deeply interested. I knew Haydon to be an admirer of Lord Byron's genius, and of his exer-

tions in favour of the Greeks. Of his lady he says,
" There is a lambent sorrow about her, bland and
touching; but she was no more fit for him than a
dove for a volcano. Poor Lady Byron! she looks
as if she *saw* an inward sorrow. Perhaps his sublime head is always haunting her imagination, like
the ' *Dira facies*' in Virgil." When he painted
Lady Byron in her place in the picture, she was
accompanied by Mrs. Jameson, and wished her to
be shewn all his drawings; but, being anxious to
paint the head in first, he considered the request to
be thoughtless, and declined till after this sitting.
This annoyed the fair illustrator of the Popish
saints, who found fault with the head. On Lady
Byron looking significantly at Mrs. Jameson, Haydon said, " Come don't *look* criticism," which he says
" annoyed her more." He made a drawing of the
head of Lloyd Garrison for the Duchess of Sutherland, and sketched Miss Knight.

The large picture was now proceeding rapidly to

completion : Haydon complains of the intrusiveness and inquisitiveness of the Americans, and of the trouble he had to parry them, except Mr. Garrison, who informed him, during one of his sittings, of his calling on and seeing the Duchess of Sutherland, with whom he was delighted. " Household and Duchess," says Haydon, " bewildered his republican faculties." He next added the head of Mr. Gurney to the group, and says, " Such a number of honest heads were never seen before, in one picture; so said the Duchess of Sutherland, and so say I." The accomplished, amiable, and fickle Amelia Opie came next, and he records her sitting, as " a very pleasant hour and a half;" and at another sitting describes her as " a delightful creature." Then came Messrs. Birney and Alexander, " both fine heads, and good hearts." Birney said, " Negro children are equal to the whites till the age of seven, when, perceiving the degradation of their parents, they felt degraded and cowed." Dreadful ! Birney had discharged all his slaves. "These delegates" he affirms to be "extraordinary men in head, feature and principle."

The above psychological fact of the connate intellect of negro children, till dismayed by dawning reason showing them the degradation of themselves and their race, is worthy of all attention, and is proved over and over again in the preceding pages.

Elihu Burritt also sat, "a keen clever fellow," also Sir Eardley Wilmot, Dr. Lushington, Messrs. Knibb, Turnbull, Moorsom and Crewdson; the latter delegate came from Birmingham in the morning, sat three hours, and returned home in the evening.

In the year 1841, the great picture of the antislavery convention was brought to a close, and exhibited. I was at the private view, as I had been of all Haydon's exhibitions; this was crowded by nobility, gentry, clergy, delegates in drab,

"Buttoned to the chin,"
Broad-cloth without, and a warm heart within,"

ladies of rank, male and female friends. This was

x

the last time I saw Mrs. Opie, (with whom I was slightly acquainted in her husband's life time,) and Mr. Clarkson, either there or at Haydon's gallery.

Previous to the exhibition of this extraordinary picture—for extraordinary it is, whether considered as a work of art, or as a faithful record of the outward lineaments and characteristics of a band of brethren, united in a great act of love to mankind —sitters who had claims for insertion poured in so fast, that to use his own expression, "at last the picture threatened to become nothing but heads, without room for bodies."

The most interesting circumstance in connection with the anti-slavery convention picture, was the visit that Haydon paid to Mr. Clarkson, at his seat in Suffolk. He left London on the 6th of April, 1841, by a steam ship, arrived at Ipswich on the 8th, found Mr. Clarkson's carriage waiting, reached Playford Hall at 8 in the evening, "found the dear old man at tea with his wife and niece, looking much better than when in town. Playford," he says, "is a fine old building; 1593, the last date, but they say it must be much older. It is surrounded by a moat, with running water. Clarkson has a head like a patriarch, and, in his prime, must have been a noble figure."

Mr. Clarkson was much pleased with a letter he had recently received from M. Guizot, then at the head of the French government, informing him that Marshal Soult, the minister for foreign affairs, and himself, intended to bring in a law for the abolition of slavery the following year.

At the sitting conversation Clarkson said,* "When Christophe's wife and daughters, all accomplished women, were brought or introduced by him to Wilberforce and others in high life, there was a sort of shrink at admitting them into society." Haydon told him he believed it, because when he proposed the African delegate in front of his picture on the same level as the Europeans, there was the same

---

* Haydon's *Autobiography*, vol. iii., p. 156.

delicacy. "But," writes Haydon, "I got him and put him in at once. Shame prevented remonstrance." "Clarkson," he again observes, "showed no envy. He spoke of Granville Sharp and Wilberforce with affection and respect; but *they* thought of the *slave*, *I*, of the *slave-trade*." A true and admirable distinction, as the whole history of its abolition proves.

During this sitting Mr. Clarkson related the whole story of his vision, of which many versions and amplifications had gone abroad. "He said he was sleeping, when a voice awoke him, and he heard distinctly the words, 'You have not done all your work; there is America.' Clarkson said it was vivid, he sat upright in his bed, he listened and heard no more. Then the whole subject of his last pamphlet* came into his mind, and texts without number crowded in. He rose in the morning, began it, and worked eight hours a day till it was com-

---

* That is, the last pamphlet that he published, so caused.

pleted; and he hoped he had not left the Americans a leg to stand on."

The physical cause of this vision, may have been that Mr. Clarkson, having thought, slightly perhaps, on the continuation of slavery in the United States of America, might have his sleeping body affected by a powerful feeling or reverie, such as has been called the *hallucinatio studiosa;* such as that in which Petrarch found himself in that minute narrative of a vision, in which Laura appeared to him; and Tasso in the lofty conversations he held with a spirit which glided towards him on the beams of the sun; or Lord Herbert of Cherbury, who, doubtful as to the propriety of publishing a work he had just finished, relates that one fair day in summer, his casement opening to the south, the sun shining clear and no wind stirring, "I took," he says, "my book, *De Veritate,* in my hand, and kneeling devoutly on my knees, said these words, 'O Thou eternal GOD! author of the light which now shines upon me, and giver of all inward illuminations, I do beseech Thee, of Thine infinite goodness, to pardon a greater request than a sinner ought to make. I am not satisfied enough whether I shall publish this book, *De Veritate*; if it be for Thy glory, I beseech Thee to give me some sign from heaven, if not, I shall suppress it.' I had no sooner spoke these words, but a loud, though gentle, voice came from the heavens, for it was like nothing on earth, which did so comfort and cheer me, that I took my petition as granted, and that I had the sign demanded."

Haydon, authorized, perhaps, by the Seer, inclines to the spiritual cause, and that there is much reality in such instances of ideal visions.* "Clarkson," he says, "has evidently been a great instrument for the abolition of a great curse. A whole species who have suffered for centuries, have, by his

---

* Mr. D'Israeli, in his *History of Men of Genius*, ch. xii., p. 188, says, "The moveable nerves of a man of genius are a reality; he sees, he hears, he feels with each. How mysterious to us is the operation of this faculty!"

exertions and those of others, been advanced in the
scale of human beings, to liberty and protection.
Is such a cause unworthy the interference of the
Deity? If not, is it improbable he would select
for such a benevolent purpose, a human being as his
instrument? The men who do these great things,
*universally*, have the impression that they are so
impelled. For instance, Columbus believed he
heard a voice in the storm, encouraging him to
persevere. Socrates believed in his attendant
spirit; and if it be allowed to refer to Christ, the
Saviour always talked of an immediate communication. I myself have believed in such communi-
cations all my life."

On the 27th of April, Haydon put the finishing
touch to this great commemorative picture, by in-
scribing upon the curtains the names of Wilberforce
and Toussaint. It was then removed to the Egyp-
tian Hall, Piccadilly, for exhibition, with the original
drawings of the heads; and on the first of May, the

month of the annual convocation of the Society of
Friends from all parts of the world, was opened to
the public.

John Beaumont wrote to the painter, complaining
of the inscriptions on the curtains, saying "they had
nothing whatever to do with the convention, and
must *come out.*" The indignant artist entered the
offending letter in his diary, and adds, "The gratitude of posterity! Without Wilberforce, Toussaint
or Sharp, no convention would have been held on
the subject. And here is my friend Beaumont in-
sisting on their names, introduced merely in allusion to their services, being struck out."

Haydon was wrong in the selection of the names,
which is surprizing, considering his recent and
numerous conferences with Mr. Clarkson on the
subject. The names, if any, to be inscribed on the
curtains of the convention, should have been the
three distinguished patriarchs of the abolition, in the
order of their precedence :—

## Sharp, Clarkson, Wilberforce,

and the motto might have been,

NEC TIMERE NEC TEMNERE.

The last act of Thomas Clarkson's public life, was his appearance at the Bar of the House of Peers, to present a petition against the slave-grown sugar bill. He passed the rest of his long and useful life at his patrimonial seat, Playford Hall, in domestic and spiritual peace and comfort.

These three distinguished leaders in one of the most righteous acts that gilds the British name, left their earthly tabernacles and a grateful world, for incorruptible crowns of eternal glory.

They took their departure from amongst us in the following order :—

---

* *Livy*, lib. vi.

GRANVILLE SHARP, on the 10th of July, 1813, aged 79.

WILLIAM WILBERFORCE, on the 29th of July, 1833, aged 79.

THOMAS CLARKSON, on the 26th of September, 1846, aged 87.

"THEY WERE LOVELY AND PLEASANT IN THEIR LIVES, AND IN THEIR DEATH THEY WERE NOT DIVIDED."

FINIS.

# CONTENTS.

# 316 CONTENTS.

## CHAPTER III.

# CONTENTS.